E. Samuel Mohanraj has set out to fill a needed gap with an in-depth explanation of the Word of God. His book contains a good exposition of the wounds of Christ. He has given a detailed study of the necessity and the meaning of these wounds that would be a delight to any senior researcher of the Word of God. His book will prove to be a useful resource for pastors and teachers of the Word of God. I pray that this book will be a blessing to all who read with a hunger and thirst to go beyond the surface.

—Rev. Dr. David Mohan
General Superintendent
The General Council of the Assemblies of God of India
Senior Pastor, New Life A.G. Church
Little Mount, Chennai

Power and Purpose in the Wounds of Jesus has been presented in a most interesting and insightful manner. Samuel Mohanraj has referred to many scriptural passages and related many personal experiences which have connected valuable spiritual truths.

The blessings we have received from the passion of Christ are clearly and carefully outlined, and I have found this book to be a positive message on Christ's atoning sacrifice.

Christians and non-Christians, with the aid of the Holy Spirit, should be able to easily comprehend the length, the breadth, and the height of God's love written on the pages of this book.

No doubt, much prayer and preparation were involved in the writing of the precepts and principles printed on each page of this book, and as this book is read, I believe everyone should gain a new appreciation for all that was involved in Jesus' suffering for our salvation.

—Rev. John D. Johnson
Senior Pastor, Bay Shore Assembly of God
Bay Shore, New York

Dr. Samuel Mohanraj has opened the door of deliverance in his book *Power and Purpose in the Wounds of Jesus*. The information and revelation contained in this book make the sacrifice of Christ relevant for daily breakthrough.

Dr. Mohanraj blends the Scriptures and personal insights together to unearth and reveal life-changing truths for both sinners and the body of Christ. He masterfully, yet in an easy-to-understand way, explains each specific point of the passion of Christ and how God intended it to bring freedom to every area of our lives. So much more than just eternal security, the truths unfolded in this book will destroy the physical bondages, mental strongholds, and spiritual hindrances that Satan uses to defeat the body of Christ. Christians can use it as a weapon, sinners will be converted through it, and preachers and teachers can study it to lead many into new levels of success in their spiritual lives.

Sam's passion also comes through in each chapter. Having seen his work in India, and both read his writings and listened to his ministry, I know this book is anointed to set the captives free and equip the saints to destroy the work of Satan's kingdom.

It is an honor to recommend this book to you. God bless you as you take your journey through the wounds of Jesus and experience for yourself the blessings we receive from the passion of Christ!

—FRANKIE POWELL
Senior Pastor, World Outreach Center, USA
Founder and President, Global Church Network
Apostolic Father to the Body of Christ at Large

Dr. E. Samuel Mohanraj is to be applauded for this wonderful and in-depth contribution on the passion narratives of our Lord Jesus Christ in his recent book entitled *Power and Purpose in the Wounds of Jesus*. May this book be a source of blessing to readers worldwide.

—RT. REV. DR. SOLOMON RAJAH, BD, MTH, DTH
Bishop of the Evangelical Lutheran Church in Malaysia

Amazing truths behind each of our Lord's wounds have been clearly brought out by Apostle E. Samuel Mohanraj. We are sure that this book will help the readers to love our Lord more and more. We are happy to stand with the author in accomplishing this great work.

—BABY GOH, JANE NG
APAC Ministries, Singapore

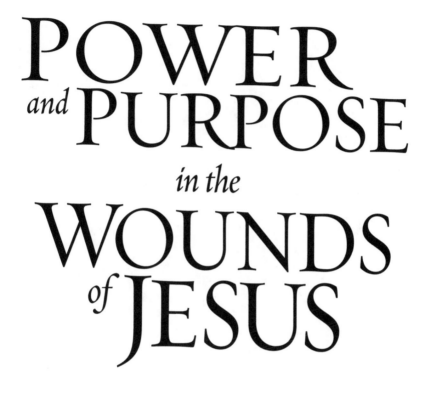

POWER
and PURPOSE
in the
WOUNDS
of JESUS

POWER
and PURPOSE
in the
WOUNDS
of JESUS

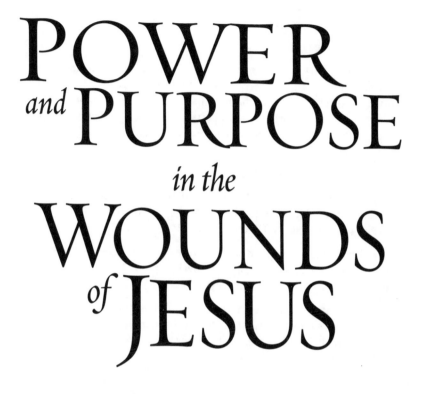

E. SAMUEL MOHANRAJ

CREATION
HOUSE
A STRANG COMPANY

POWER AND PURPOSE IN THE WOUNDS OF JESUS
by E. Samuel Mohanraj
Published by Creation House
A Strang Company
600 Rinehart Road
Lake Mary, Florida 32746
www.strangbookgroup.com

Unless otherwise stated, all Scripture quotations are taken from the King James Version of the Bible.

Scripture quotations marked NKJV are from the New King James Version of the Bible. Copyright © 1979, 1980, 1982 by Thomas Nelson, Inc., publishers. Used by permission.

Scripture quotations marked NIV are from the Holy Bible, New International Version of the Bible. Copyright © 1973, 1978, 1984, International Bible Society. Used by permission.

Scripture quotations marked AMP are from the Amplified Bible. Old Testament copyright © 1965, 1987 by the Zondervan Corporation. The Amplified New Testament copyright © 1954, 1958, 1987 by the Lockman Foundation. Used by permission.

Scripture quotations marked ASV are from the American Standard Bible. Copyright © 1960, 1962, 1968, 1971, 1972, 1973, 1975, by the Lockman Foundation. Used by permission.

Scripture quotations marked BBE are taken from Bible in Basic English.

Design Director: Bill Johnson
Cover design by Justin Evans

Library of Congress Control Number: 2009931066
International Standard Book Number: 978-1-59979-864-6

First Edition

09 10 11 12 13 — 9 8 7 6 5 4 3 2 1

Printed in the United States of America

*This book is dedicated to
the memory of our daughter
Sharon Samuel*

ACKNOWLEDGMENTS

I THANK MY LORD Jesus Christ for using me as a tool to reveal the secrets behind every wound that was inflicted on Him.

I am indebted to my wife Elizabeth, my son Mervyn Samuel, my brother Ruban, his wife Esther, my mother Bessie Ebenezer, my mother-in-law Sakkubai, and my assistant Vincent, for standing by me and supporting the ministry.

I want to seize this opportunity to thank my well-wishers, who encouraged and supported me in the work of this book, especially to Mrs. Jane Ng, Mrs. Baby Goh, Sis. Yulin, Mrs. Ramya, her husband Mr. Sadish, and Sis. Shirley Yong for their help to publish this book in America.

I am grateful to Mrs. Seline Augustine, Mr. Christie D Abishegam, Mr. C. John Victor, Pastor D. John Rajasingh and Mrs. and Mr. Steve Chulick for their valuable contributions and suggestions in writing this book.

I would like to thank my staff and well-wishers around the world for their love and support to me.

My "thank you" and appreciation also go to the staff of Creation House for their dedicated service in publishing this book.

CONTENTS

FOREWORD

THERE IS A gift of "revelation," that the apostle Paul spoke of, that can "open the eyes of understanding" to the deeper revelations found in the scriptures. This insight is often gleaned through biblical patterns, types and shadows, and understanding the meaning of Apocalyptic symbolism. Minister E. Samuel Mohanraj has received this unique gift, and this book, *Power and Purpose in the Wounds of Jesus*, will open the eyes of your understanding in a fresh way to a powerful dimension of Christ's wounds, that as a long-time Christian, you may have never heard taught before.

You will learn that the depth and mystery of our suffering Messiah, Jesus Christ, is so vast that it impacts every aspect of our lives, including emotional and personal areas that are seldom taught or understood in the church. It has taken sixteen different chapters to explore and explain this mystery—in an easy to read and comprehend fashion.

By the conclusion of this book, you will never see the sufferings of Christ the same, and your appreciation for this powerful event will be life-long!

—PERRY STONE
Host of *Manna-fest*
Founder and President of Voice of Evangelism

INTRODUCTION

A FEW YEARS AGO, due to a certain problem in my life, I felt heaviness in my heart and dejection in my spirit. During that phase, I had a vision in which our Lord showed me how He was beaten up, verbally abused, humiliated, and tortured. He also showed me the dreadful scene of Himself hanging on the cross. On seeing this vision, my heart melted like wax. Though there was sadness in my heart, I suddenly realized that our Lord had finished a great task on the cross in order to lift me up and save me from all the attacks of the devil. I also came to the realization that His suffering was meant to be not only a blessing to me, but also to all the people of this world. On understanding this truth, that heaviness left me and a sense of joy came into my heart.

I was thankful to our Lord for this wonderful vision, yet at the same time, I was wondering why He had shown it to me—a worthless and useless person. Was it just to lift me up from my state of heaviness, or was it for some other purpose? There was indeed a purpose as to why He showed this vision to me.

Prior to this, in my heart I had wondered whether I could ever see the suffering that Christ underwent when He was in this world. When I asked God whether it was possible to see His Son's suffering, the Spirit of the Lord prompted me to read the following verses from the Bible:

> For I received from the Lord that which I also delivered to you: that the Lord Jesus on the same night in

which He was betrayed took bread; and when He had given thanks, He broke it and said, "Take, eat; this is My body which is broken for you; do this in remembrance of Me." In the same manner He also took the cup after supper, saying, "This cup is the new covenant in My blood. This do, as often as you drink it, in remembrance of Me." For as often as you eat this bread and drink this cup, you proclaim the Lord's death till He comes.

—1 CORINTHIANS 11:23–26, NKJV

Any vision, dream, or prophesy should be based on the Word of God. In the above verses, Paul has written how our Lord Jesus Christ, on the day that He was betrayed, had supper with His disciples and had spoken to them. At that time Paul was not with the apostles in the upper room. In those days, when this incident happened, Paul was not even saved. Paul knew how our Lord Jesus had given communion not through any of the apostles, but by the revelation of the Lord Himself. Paul clearly recorded in his epistle to us and to the church at Corinth that the Lord Himself revealed this incident to him.

The Bible says in Acts 10:34, "God is no respecter of persons." God shows no partiality. Therefore, God is able to show us even now the things which happened during Jesus' time through visions, dreams, or any other means. Moreover, according to Acts 2:17, "And it shall come to pass in the last days, says God, that I will pour out of My Spirit on all flesh; …your young men shall see visions" (NKJV).

Even as I received this vision from our Lord, He helped me to understand the spiritual truths that are inherent in the sufferings He underwent. It is indeed amazing to know the glory and blessings one can receive through His sufferings. It was this divine inspiration that prompted me to write this book.

I encountered many tragedies when I started to write this book. The devil brought continual opposition, but God gave me the grace to overcome each trial. In December 2004, my parents came to visit me in Chennai to celebrate Christmas. Chennai is located on the southeast coast of India and was once known as Madras. This is where I now live and my ministry is based.

Early in the morning of December 28 my father, who was then seventy-five years old, was walking back to his room in a sleepy state when he suddenly slipped and rolled down the staircase, suffering a severe head injury. Hearing the commotion, we ran out of our rooms only to find my father lying in a pool of blood on the last of the steps.

Later, a person who I believe was once under the influence of the devil, explained to me that my father did not simply fall down the steps but instead was intentionally pushed by the devil. Throughout this entire ordeal, my faith did not waver and I did not stop writing this book. In fact, I could feel the supernatural strength of God flowing through me, causing my faith to grow stronger. There were many other hurdles that I faced, and I have written about them in the latter part of this book. God gave me the grace to success-fully complete this book after a period of five years for the glory of His name.

I strongly believe that before our Lord's Second Coming a mighty revival will take place all over the world (Acts 2:17). This revival will break only when we go back to the cross and preach on the sufferings of our Lord Jesus Christ and the victory He gave us. I am sure this book will be a great resource for the end-time harvest.

Beloved, I deem it a great and rare privilege to share with you deep spiritual thoughts about the description and impact of the wounds inflicted on the body of Jesus Christ, the significance of each wound, and the blessings we receive through His wounds. May our Lord help you to inherit all these blessings.

PREAMBLE

T HIS VERSE CONFIRMS the truth that wounds had to
be inflicted on the body of Jesus when He came as
our redeemer, and that those wounds would bring
us peace and healing.

Years ago, I met a very wealthy man who shared with me
how he became rich. When he was a young man he left his
village for the city of Chennai, in search of a job. Even after
several days he remained jobless, and he had to starve and
sleep on the streets.

Eventually, he got a job as a lorry cleaner. Gradually he
learned to drive a lorry and was promoted as a driver. Out
of his meager salary he saved money little by little, and, in
due course, he bought a lorry of his own. As his income
increased, he bought another lorry and then another. Thus,
by working hard day and night, he became the owner of a
fleet of lorries and invested his earnings in various businesses. When he died, he left properties worth hundreds of
thousands of dollars for his children.

However, his children never realized how hard their father
had toiled to earn the money to buy those properties. They

never knew that he once suffered starvation and lived in poverty. In fact, they were ignorant of every hardship their father had endured to make them rich. They were wasteful, spending everything they had on unnecessary luxury. They sold the properties one by one so as to live lavish lives until finally there was nothing left. Today, they are leading miserable lives, unable to make both ends meet.

Dearly beloved, because they were ignorant of the hardships their father underwent to make them rich, these children quickly squandered away the blessings that their father had gained for them. Likewise, if we are ignorant of how Jesus earned blessings for us, we too will not inherit and enjoy those blessings. When we realize the pain, suffering, shame, disgrace, accusation, and wounds He willingly faced and endured, we will be able to appreciate and experience true peace, health, and blessing.

The wounds inflicted on various parts of Jesus' body were by no means a matter of mere chance. It was the devil who caused every single wound with a specific purpose. For example, when we read in the Bible about Job it says:

> And the LORD said unto Satan, Behold, all that he hath is in thy power; only upon himself put not forth thine hand. So Satan went forth from the presence of the LORD.
>
> —JOB 1:12

Satan departed from the presence of the Lord and brought ruin in the life of Job. The Sabeans plundered his oxen. The Chaldeans carried away his camels. Fire from heaven consumed his sheep and servants. A great wind from the wilderness killed all his sons and daughters. One after another these things happened to Job, all on the same day (Job 1:13–19).

Satan selected one day and brought ruin into the life of Job by making use of the Sabeans, Chaldeans and also fire and strong wind. He completed his plan of ruining the happy existence of Job by using people and nature as his tools or agents.

In the same way, Satan, the ruler of this world, planned to destroy Jesus Christ, the Son of the Living God. When He was in the womb of Virgin Mary, the devil worked in the mind of Joseph (who was betrothed to Mary) to put her away secretly. According to Jewish law, if a woman was not a virgin when she was married, she was to be stoned to death (Deut. 22:21). However, the Lord spoke to Joseph to accept her and protect her (Matt. 1:18–25). Had Joseph not done this, Mary and her baby would have died.

After Jesus was born to Mary according to the plan of God, the devil started working on King Herod. He incited him to kill all male children of two years old and under. But the angel of the Lord appeared to Joseph in a dream and instructed him to flee to Egypt (Matt. 2:13). Once again we see that the devil's plan was thwarted by God.

In another incident, Satan filled the minds of those listening to Jesus' preaching, with seething anger. Satan provoked them to try to cast Jesus down from the brow of the steep hill on which their city was built (Luke 4:29–30). But our Lord passed through them and they could do nothing to Him. Yet another time He created in the minds of some people a desire to stone Him to death. Here again Jesus passed through them unhurt (John 8:59; 10:31–39). Every one of these wicked designs of the devil failed miserably.

Only when Judas betrayed Jesus in the garden of Gethsemane did He willingly surrender Himself to the servants of the high priest. Thus, only then and in accordance with God's divine plan did the devil's scheme *seem* "victorious."

Satan had a plan and purpose for each of the wounds inflicted on the body of Jesus. What Satan intended for evil, God turned into good as He always does. Satan was indeed goaded to take revenge on God, but he got entangled in his own ploy, and all those plans were thwarted by the blood of Jesus. In fact, Satan's evil plan of destruction had the radically opposite effect of bringing peace, blessings, healing, and joy to all those who accepted Jesus as Lord and Savior. These spiritual truths will bring great blessings in your life.

Chapter 1
WOUNDS BY THE CROWN OF THORNS

And when they had platted a crown of thorns, they put it upon
his head, and a reed in his right hand: and they bowed the knee
before him, and mocked him, saying, Hail, King of the Jews!
—MATTHEW 27:29

A GORY TOOL OF torture that Jesus endured at the hands of the Roman soldiers was the crown of thorns. Historians describe the crown as woven of small flexible branches covered with long thorns. These thorns were very strong, extremely sharp, and capable of making deep wounds.

We have already seen that it is actually Satan who intentionally inflicted every wound on Jesus, and the Roman soldiers were only his agents. Being known as a killer and destroyer (John 10:10), Satan could not have shown the least mercy on Jesus. Therefore, the pricks caused by Satan on Jesus could not have been light at all.

There must have been profuse bleeding when the soldiers placed the crown upon His head and the thorns penetrated His scalp. In fact, the thorns in the crown should have caused excruciating pain all over Jesus' head. And each subsequent blow on Jesus' head would have driven the thorns deeper and deeper (Matt. 27:30; Mark 15:19). The crown of thorns would have been on Jesus' head until He died on the cross because the Scripture is silent about its removal. Though the soldiers did this to mock Jesus, there is a spiritual meaning behind what happened.

Thorns Are a Symbol of Curse

Genesis 3:13–18 describes God's response to the temptation of the devil through the serpent and the subsequent disobedience of Adam and Eve when they ate the forbidden fruit.

God speaks to the serpent:

> And the LORD God said unto the serpent, Because thou hast done this, thou art cursed above all cattle, and above every beast of the field; upon thy belly shalt thou go, and dust shalt thou eat all the days of thy life.
> —Genesis 3:14

Later God addresses Adam:

> And unto Adam He said, Because thou hast hearkened unto the voice of thy wife, and hast eaten of the tree, of which I commanded thee saying, Thou shalt not eat of it: cursed is the ground for thy sake; in sorrow shalt thou eat of it all the days of thy life; Thorns also and thistles shall it bring forth to thee; and thou shalt eat the herb of the field.
> —Genesis 3:17–18

God saw that each of His creation was good, but after He created Adam and said that it was not good that man should be alone, He made a helpmeet (suitable help) for him. And after God created man and woman in His own image and likeness, the Scripture says He blessed them:

> And God blessed them, and God said unto them, Be
> fruitful, and multiply, and replenish the earth, and
> subdue it: and have dominion over the fish of the sea,
> and over the fowl of the air, and over every living thing
> that moveth upon the earth.
>
> —GENESIS 1:28

We can see from the first two chapters of Genesis that what God created was good and blessed, not cursed. Only after the disobedience of Adam and Eve did God pronounce a curse. The curse came as a result of evil and sin introduced into His creation.

The first curse that God pronounced was on the serpent. Later God cursed the land, not Adam and Eve, as a result of their disobedience. Remember in verse 18, God said of the land, "Thorns also and thistles shall it bring forth to thee." The New American Standard Bible says that "thorns and thistles shall grow." This means that thorns and thistles will spring forth.

Hebrews 6:7–8 says, "For the earth which drinks in the rain that often comes upon it, and bears herbs useful for those by whom it is cultivated, receives blessing from God; but if it bears thorns and briars, it is rejected and near to being cursed, whose end is to be burned" (NKJV). This scripture clearly says that if the ground yields thorns and thistles it is cursed. Therefore, we could say that thorns are a result of the curse.

Since the first curse was given to Satan, and because thorns were a result of the curse on the land, Satan wanted to give those thorns back to Jesus, the Son of God and Creator of heaven and Earth. He was taking revenge on God for punishing him.

It was not a common practice to place a crown of thorns on the head of a condemned man about to be crucified. The two thieves, who died on either side of Jesus, did not have crowns of thorns placed on their heads.

But Satan induced the Roman soldiers to put the crown of thorns on Jesus' head after He responded, "It is as you say" to Pilate's question, "Are you the King of the Jews?" (Matt. 27:11). Satan must have been laughing and enjoying himself over this apparent symbolic 'victory.' He was probably thinking that he had finally given back the curse to the One who cursed him.

We know that sin was born in Satan, who in turn, influenced Adam and Eve to disobey God. The Bible says of Lucifer:

> How art thou fallen from heaven, O Lucifer, son of the morning! how art thou cut down to the ground, which didst weaken the nations! For thou hast said in thine heart, I will ascend into heaven, I will exalt my throne above the stars of God: I will sit also upon the mount of the congregation, in the sides of the north: I will ascend above the heights of the clouds; I will be like the most High.
>
> —ISAIAH 14:12–14

No one seduced Lucifer to desire to ascend into heaven to sit upon the mount of the congregation. No one asked him to ascend above the heights of the clouds to be like the most High. The sin of pride was born within Lucifer.

Adam and Eve would never have eaten the forbidden fruit if Lucifer had not tempted them, because sin was not born within them. But because of Satan's influence they disobeyed God and ate the forbidden fruit.

4

That is why I presume that God wanted to save human-kind. Jesus bore the crown of thorns willingly in order to save human beings from every curse, including the curse as the outcome of sin. The One who pronounced the curse had taken the curse on Himself in order to bless all of humanity.

HOW CURSES ARE INVOKED

From the Bible we can see that a curse can come upon us in four different ways.

Disobedience to God's Word

First, when a person disobeys God's commands the curses listed in Deuteronomy 28:15–68 will come upon him or her.

One example is that of King Saul. He disobeyed God's Word and offered the burnt offering himself instead of waiting for the prophet Samuel (1 Sam. 13:9–14). He eventually lost his kingdom.

I once knew a man who was a hard worker and who also had a loving and lovely wife. He had a talent for organizing and conducting business exhibitions. As his reputation grew, businesses hired him to exhibit their products. Soon he became very successful and was earning lots of money.

But I noticed that within a week of one of his shows, all of his money was gone. When he had money he would travel by airplane. When he lost his money he would hitchhike from place to place. I could not understand how he could lose all of his money in a week's time.

Then one day I found out that he was leading an adulterous life. His wife left him and soon his business began to fail. Then his father died and his sisters had problems in their marriages. This man's sinful lifestyle, disobedience to God's law, had brought curses on him and his family.

5

Sin of forefathers

Secondly, Exodus 34:7 says that God "...by no means clearing the guilty, visiting the iniquity of the fathers upon the children and the children's children to the third and the fourth generation." In other words, because of the sins of one's forefathers, a person may have a generational curse in his or her life.

Many years ago there was a man holding a large sum of money from the sale of his property. The man was reluctant to travel at night, fearing that someone might rob him on the way. So he accepted the invitation of a friend to stay at his lodge for a night.

During the night the friend killed the man and took all the money. Everyone in the city knew that the friend was the murderer, but because he was a very influential person no one was willing to report the matter to the police.

After some time the "friend" was afflicted with leprosy. As the years passed, one by one his children and then his grandchildren got leprosy. The leprosy was the result of this man's sin. Due to the sin of their forefather, the descendants suffered from a generational curse.

Curse due to the words of our enemies

Thirdly, someone pronouncing a curse on a person can bring a curse in the person's life. That is why the Moabite king was willing to pay the prophet Balaam to curse his enemy, the Israelites (Num. 22:5–6).

I remember the story of a very successful businessman I know. One day he had severe chest pain and was admitted in the hospital. A team of doctors examined him thoroughly, but could not find any reason for the sickness.

When I heard that he was in the hospital, I went to pray

for him. During our conversation I discovered that he was suffering from oppression of a spirit resulting from the words spoken against him by a jealous competitor. When we prayed, God delivered him from this curse, and today this man continues to flourish in his career.

In the Bible, Laban asked Jacob why he had stolen the idols from his house. Jacob, not knowing that his wife Rachel had taken them said, "With whomever you find your gods, do not let him live" (Gen. 31:32, NKJV). I believe this may be why Rachel died while giving birth to Benjamin. In the same way, curses delivered by parents or anyone else may bring a curse upon someone.

Self curse

Fourthly, a person can bring a curse upon himself by his own words. Proverbs 18:21 tells us that, "Death and life are in the power of the tongue: and they that love it shall eat the fruit thereof." Out of frustration or even ignorance, a person may speak negative words of death over his own life, and this can bring a curse upon himself by his own words.

Several years ago a man asked me to pray for his failing business. As I began to pray the Holy Spirit prompted me to ask him how he spoke to his employees. Surprised by the question, the man reluctantly admitted that whenever he got frustrated, he used to call his workers "idiots."

I explained to him that the negative words spoken over his employees were like pronouncing a curse on them, and eventually this curse affected the success of his business.

Another example of self-curse is that of Judas. After betraying Jesus with a kiss in the garden, Judas realized that he had sinned and betrayed innocent blood. Instead of repenting for his actions, he hanged himself (Matt. 27:4–5).

I believe that Judas pronounced a curse on himself which led to his committing suicide.

Thus, a curse can come upon us because of our disobedience to the Word of God, because of the sins of our forefathers, because someone pronounces a curse on us, or because we curse ourselves.

But rest assured that in whatever forms the curse may come there is no need to worry because the blood, which Jesus shed from the crown of thorns, has the power to remove any curse. Jesus became the curse to remove the curse in your life (Gal. 3:13).

Thorns are a symbol of pain

In 2 Corinthians 12:7 the Apostle Paul writes:

> And lest I should be exalted above measure through the abundance of the revelations, there was given to me a thorn in the flesh, the messenger of Satan to buffet me, lest I should be exalted above measure.

Here Paul mentions "a thorn in the flesh." While it is not very clear what the thorn in Paul's flesh was, I do know from my own experience that anytime a thorn pierces my flesh it definitely causes physical pain.

Anyone who loves roses would know that those beautiful, often fragrant flowers appear on prickly branches whose thorns are sharp and prone to penetrate the flesh. I know, too, that if the thorn is not removed immediately it will continue to cause pain.

I know of a lady who suffered from migraines for many years. For her the sharp pain was like a thorn penetrating her head. But when she was prayed for, she was instantly healed.

Yes, Jesus knows very well the physical pain that a thorn

8

can cause to the head. Jesus accepted the crown of thorns and the pain associated with it in order to heal every kind of sickness.

We can also say that the thorn can cause emotional pain. For example, when we are pierced with a thorn, our immediate response is shock and maybe even anger. Our attention is turned quickly to the area of pain. While proofreading an early manuscript for this book, my son Mervyn made an interesting observation. He said that while there is pain in our body all of our attention is focused on that area. And of course, when we focus on the pain, we no longer focus on God and His blessings.

I know of a young man who fell in love and was about to marry his fiancée. But shortly before the wedding, his fiancée left him for a wealthy man. At first the young man was shocked at his girlfriend's betrayal. Then he became very angry.

Her action caused great emotional pain in his life. Because of this he stopped going to church and reverted to a worldly lifestyle. But one day the Lord touched his heart and healed his emotional wounds. God gave him a wonderful wife, and now he is a blessed man.

Isaiah 53:5 says:

> But he was wounded for our transgressions, he was bruised for our iniquities: the chastisement of our peace was upon him; and with his stripes we are healed.

The blood, which Jesus shed from the crown of thorns, has the power not only to remove curses from our lives, but also has the power to heal any physical or emotional pain and sickness in our lives.

When you begin to praise Him, thank Him and trust Him,

believing that He bore your suffering, sickness and pain, you can be healed.

Thorns are a symbol of worry

In the parable of the sower Jesus said:

> And these are they which are sown among thorns; such as hear the word. And the cares of this world, and the deceitfulness of riches, and the lusts of other things entering in, choke the word, and it becometh unfruitful.
>
> —MARK 4:18–19

During this teaching Jesus mentions that some of the seeds fell by the wayside, some on stony ground, some among the thorns, and some on the good ground.

He goes on to explain that the seeds which fell among the thorns refer to those who, through the cares of this world and deceitfulness of riches and the lusts of other things entering in, allow the Word of God to become unfruitful in their lives.

Here we can clearly see that thorns are a symbol of the cares of this world or, in other words, worry. In Matthew 6:25–34, Jesus Himself addresses the subject of worry. He tells us not to worry about the cares of this world like what we shall eat, what we shall drink, or what we shall wear. He reminds us that our heavenly Father already knows that we need all of these things.

He asks us to seek first the kingdom of God and His righteousness and all these things will be added to us (Matt. 6:33). His conclusion is to take no thought for tomorrow for "each day has enough trouble of its own" (Matt. 6:34, NIV). One of Satan's principal weapons against God's children is bringing worry into their lives. He knows that worry leads to fear, and that fear is the opposite of faith (Mark 4:40). Where fear operates, faith cannot operate, and without faith it is impossible to please God.

Hebrews 11:6 says:

> But without faith it is impossible to please him: for he that cometh to God must believe that he is, and that he is a rewarder of them that diligently seek him.

When our faith is reduced by fear we are unable to please God, and we are no longer able to receive blessings from Him. Remember, it takes faith to "believe that He is and that He is a rewarder of them who diligently seek Him."

Satan knows that this chain reaction of worry leads to fear, and fear reduces our faith, and diverts our attention away from God and His promises. Worry prevents us from seeing and believing the wonderful plan that God has for us.

Proverbs 12:25 says:

> Heaviness in the heart of man maketh it stoop.

Where there is worry there is heaviness in the heart, and heaviness in the heart makes a person stoop. One of the definitions of *stoop* is "to descend from a superior position." Worrying about your future or about your children's future is a form of doubt and unbelief. This may deter you from receiving God's blessings. The Bible makes it clear that we should cast our burden upon Him:

> Cast thy burden upon the Lord, and he shall sustain thee: he shall never suffer the righteous to be moved.
> —PSALM 55:22

11

Casting all your care upon him; for he careth for you.
—1 PETER 5:7

There was a woman who was married at a very young age. After a year she gave birth to a baby girl. Soon after, her husband abandoned her for another woman. Without a job and with little education she turned to her father for help in raising her daughter. But soon her father died and she was left all alone.

Penniless and worried about her future, she turned to Jesus. Suddenly the lives of this lady and her daughter were in the hands of our loving Savior. Jesus took away her worry and guaranteed their future. Today this lady is as blessed as Naomi.

Jesus' blood shed from the crown of thorns has the power to take away the worry from your mind.

Thorns are a symbol of the deceitfulness of riches

In the previous section we referred to the parable of the sower. In Mark 4:18-19 Jesus said, "And these are they which are sown among thorns; such as hear the word, and the cares of this world, and the deceitfulness of riches, and the lusts of other things entering in, choke the word, and it becometh unfruitful." Here we learn that thorns are also a symbol of the deceitfulness of riches.

In Mark 10:17, the rich young ruler knelt before Jesus and asked, "Good Master, what shall I do that I may inherit eternal life?"

Jesus responded, "Thou knowest the commandments, Do not commit adultery, Do not kill, Do not steal, Do not bear false witness, Defraud not, Honour thy father and mother."

The young man answered saying, "Master, all these have I observed from my youth."

Then Jesus loving him and said, "One thing thou lackest: go thy way, sell whatsoever thou hast, and give to the poor, and thou shalt have treasure in heaven: and come, take up the cross, and follow me."

But the young man was sad at that reply, and went away grieved, for he had great possessions (Mark 10:18–22).

Even though he spoke to Jesus face to face, this young man could not enter the kingdom of God. His great possessions became a thorn of deceitfulness of riches, causing him to think only of his life on earth.

I know of a gentleman who is an elder in his local church. He loves God and is very generous in giving his time and money to the work of the Lord. One day he had a heart attack, and I went to the hospital to pray with him. As I began to pray, the Holy Spirit told me that this man was cheating the government by not paying his taxes.

When I asked him about this, he tried to convince me that there was nothing wrong in what he was doing because the money he thus saved by not paying taxes was actually being used to advance the kingdom of God. I told him that this was wrong and that even Jesus paid his taxes. I explained that God does not approve of cheating the government in order to support the local church. This church elder's stubbornness during the discussion revealed that his love of money was much more than his love of the Lord.

God wants to bless us and certainly knows what is best for us, but some people insist on conducting their lives in their own ways, trusting in the things of this world like their own possessions and resources. That is deceitfulness of riches.

The ruler of this world has blinded the eyes and hardened the hearts of some people, making it impossible for them to see and understand God's heart (2 Cor. 4:4). But the blood that Jesus shed from the wounds near His eyes caused by the crown of thorns can help us to see the light of the gospel of the glory of Christ. His blood has set our minds free so that we can receive the things of God and trust in Him alone rather than in the things of this world.

Thorns are a symbol of the lusts of other things

Referring again to the parable of the sower in Mark 4:18–19, Jesus said, "And these are they which are sown among thorns; such as hear the word, and the cares of this world, and the deceitfulness of riches, and the lusts of other things entering in, choke the word, and it becometh unfruitful." Here we can see that thorns are also a symbol of the lusts of other things.

> For all that is in the world, the lust of the flesh, and the lust of the eyes, and the pride of life, is not of the Father, but is of the world.
>
> —1 JOHN 2:16

The lust of other things is actually the lust of the flesh or the pleasures of this life. Lust is the carnal desire of objects which are pleasing to the sensual mind. It is the world of sense overcoming the world of spirit.

First Peter 4:2–3 (NKJV) reminds us:

> That he no longer should live the rest of his time in the flesh for the lusts of men, but for the will of God. For we have spent enough of our past lifetime in doing the will of the Gentiles—when we walked in lewdness, lusts, drunkenness, revelries, drinking parties, and abominable idolatries.

14

I recently heard the testimony of a man who was infected with AIDS. He was sitting alone in a train compartment late one night when a prostitute enticed him into an adulterous relationship. Now, not only does he have an incurable disease, but he has also lost his wife, family, and job. In essence he traded for a few moments of pleasure the destruction of a lifetime.

Many people become addicted to things such as alcohol, drugs, and pornography and cannot easily get rid of them. But the blood of Jesus shed from the crown of thorns can deliver you and heal you.

Satan would have thought that he paid back God by placing the crown of thorns, a symbol of curse, on Jesus. But God knows exactly what these wounds in the head of Jesus are going to do in our lives.

Our Lord not only took the curse, but He also took all our pains, worries, and agony that come due to the deceitfulness of riches and the lust of other things. "Surely He has borne our griefs and carried our sorrows; yet we esteemed Him stricken, smitten by God, and afflicted" (Isa. 53:4).

The blood that Jesus shed from the wounds resulting from the crown of thorns also covered the crown of thorns. His blood still covers those things that the thorns represent in our lives.

Chapter 2
WOUNDS ON HIS HEAD

Then the soldiers of the governor took Jesus into the common hall, and
gathered unto him the whole band of soldiers. And they stripped him, and
put on him a scarlet robe. And when they had platted a crown of thorns,
they put it upon his head, and a reed in his right hand: and they bowed
the knee before him, and mocked him, saying, Hail, King of the Jews!
And they spit upon him, and took the reed, and smote him on the head.

—MATTHEW 27:27–30

BEGINNING WITH ADAM and Eve in the Garden of Eden and throughout history, the devil has been trying to convince people that the Word of God is not true.

In Genesis 3:1–5, the serpent said to the woman, "Yea, hath God said, Ye shall not eat of every tree of the garden?" Eve replied, "We may eat of the fruit of the trees of the garden: But of the fruit of the tree which is in the midst of the garden, God hath said, Ye shall not eat of it, neither shall ye touch it, lest ye die." And the serpent said to the woman, "Ye shall not surely die: For God doth know that in the day ye eat thereof, then your eyes shall be opened, and ye shall be as gods, knowing good and evil."

Satan continues to use this same strategy today, deceiving people with his lies and causing them to doubt the truth of

God's Word. Sadly, many people just like Eve believe these lies, which leave them feeling lonely, rejected, and forgotten.

After the Roman soldiers put the crown of thorns on Jesus' head, the Scripture says, they took the reed and smote Him on the head. The Greek word for *reed* is *kalamos* (kal'-am-os) and can also be translated as "staff." Is not the king's scepter a thick rod? The NIV Bible says that the Roman soldiers took the staff and struck Jesus on his head again and again (Matt. 27:30). The prophet Micah also prophesied that the ruler of Israel would be struck with the rod (Mic. 5:1–2).

Therefore it is evident that the reed they used was not a tall blade of grass with a hollow stem, but rather a thick rod that was capable of striking a heavy blow. In fact, the Greek word for *smote* is *tupto* (toop'-to) and it means to strike or beat with a staff, a whip or the fist.

Jesus already had the crown of thorns on His head when the soldiers started beating Him with the reed. The impact of each blow would have injured His head and also caused the thorns that pierced His scalp to be driven deeper and deeper. No doubt there was tremendous bleeding.

WHY DID THEY INFLICT WOUNDS TO HIS HEAD?

Several years ago a friend of mine was traveling in India at night by a motorcycle. As he took a sharp turn, he failed to notice a buffalo lying on the road. His motorcycle struck the animal, and he went flying through the air. The impact of landing on the hard ground caused multiple fractures and a severe head injury to my friend.

My friend was immediately taken to the hospital where the best doctors in the city attended on him. He quickly recovered from the fractures, but because of the severe head injury he could not remember anything; he lost all memory of his past.

This was the devil's intention in making the soldiers take the reed and smite Jesus on the head. He wanted them to inflict severe injury to His head so that it would cause Jesus to lose His memory.

Satan knows that Jesus Christ is the Son of God and the Word made flesh. He wanted to make Jesus forget His past and where He came from. He wanted Jesus to forget His people and the promises of God for them. If he could accomplish this, then it would prove that the Word of God is not true.

The Bible says that after they put the crown of thorns on His head and beat Him with the reed, the soldiers brought Jesus back to Pontius Pilate. Pilate asked Him, "Where are you from? But Jesus gave him no answer" (John 19:9, NKJV). At that point the devil was probably laughing and thinking that Jesus had lost His memory.

But when Pilate insisted on a reply from Jesus, telling Him "Speakest thou not unto me? Knowest thou not that I have power to crucify thee, and have power to release thee?" Jesus responded, "Thou couldest have no power at all against me, except it were given thee from above: therefore he that delivered me unto thee hath the greater sin" (John 19:10–11).

In spite of the injuries from the blows to the head, the crown of thorns, and loss of blood, Jesus still remembered from where He had come and the purpose for which He was sent.

Moreover, the Bible says, "When Jesus therefore saw his mother, and the disciple standing by, whom he loved, he saith unto his mother, Woman, behold thy son! Then saith he to the disciple, Behold thy mother! And from that hour that disciple took her unto his own home" (John 19:26–27). Even when He was hanging on the cross, Jesus did not forget His mother and His disciple.

The wounds to Jesus' head were intended by Satan to make Him forget us. But Jesus defeated the devil's plan and proved beyond doubt that God's Word is true and that He will never forget us.

From the time I was a young man I had a desire to travel abroad. For many years I thought my athletic ability would enable me to represent my country internationally. But my sports career remained a mere dream due to an injury. When I accepted Jesus Christ, I cried out to God saying, "Lord, I know that I will come to heaven when I die. At least in my spirit take me around the world before I come to heaven." Since I was a fledgling Christian at that time, I prayed liked that. After that I totally forgot this prayer.

Years later, to do God's ministry I had to take an airplane from the city of Kuala Lumpur, Malaysia, to Tokyo, Japan. From there I traveled to Los Angles, California, and then on to New York. After that I was off to Dubai, UAE, and then finally back to Kuala Lumpur.

As soon as I landed at the airport in Kuala Lumpur, the Holy Spirit spoke to me saying, "Son, I just took you all the way around the world." I suddenly remembered the prayer I said years ago. Though I had forgotten all about it, the one true living God did not. He remembered and fulfilled the desires of my heart.

As I mentioned in the Introduction, my father fell down the steps in my home and this resulted in a head injury. While the doctors were examining him they pointed to my mother and asked my father to identify her. He said that he did not know her. On hearing this, my mother felt shattered because of my father's failure to recognize her after fifty years of marriage, sharing all the joys and sorrows of life with my father.

Once I went to an old age home for the shooting of a Tamil video song for our television program. All the old folks were excited that they were going to be featured in a television program. While shooting, I asked an old lady to perform a particular action. It did not come out the way we expected. So I asked her to do it again. Even after four attempts, it did not come out well. I felt bad to ask her to repeat it. On seeing my face, she volunteered to perform once again. She said, "My children have totally forgotten me. Now, at least on seeing me in the television they will remember me and pay me a visit." She added, "Though I am tired, I will fully co-operate with you for this particular role." The next shot came out very well and she was able to perform to our expectation. Her words of agony still ring in my ears.

My dear readers, those whom you have loved may forget you. Those who have made promises to help you may forget you. Even your own parents or children may forget you. Perhaps you think that God has forgotten you just like Gideon did.

I want to encourage you that the blood which Jesus shed from the wounds to His head, the same blood that washes away your sin, will also wash away your loneliness. The devil wants you to think that Jesus has forgotten you. But God's Word says that He will never forget you (Deut. 31:6) and God's Word is always true.

Numbers 23:19 says, "God is not a man, that he should lie; neither the son of man, that he should repent: hath he said, and shall he not do it? or hath he spoken, and shall he not make it good?" When God makes a promise, He will certainly fulfill it. In Matthew 24:35, Jesus promises, "Heaven and earth shall pass away, but my words shall not pass away."

He who promised is faithful.

—HEBREWS 10:23, NKJV

...what he had promised, he was able also to perform.

—ROMANS 4:21, NKJV

The Bible is full of promises that our Lord will never forget us. Here are a few examples to remind, comfort, and encourage you today.

Can a woman forget her sucking child, that she should not have compassion on the son of her womb? yea, they may forget, yet will I not forget thee.

—ISAIAH 49:15

(For the LORD thy God is a merciful God;) he will not forsake thee, neither destroy thee, nor forget the covenant of thy fathers which he sware unto them.

—DEUTERONOMY 4:31

When the poor and needy seek water, and there is none, and their tongue faileth for thirst, I the LORD will hear them, I the God of Israel will not forsake them.

—ISAIAH 41:17

Remember these, O Jacob and Israel; for thou art my servant: I have formed thee; thou art my servant: O Israel, thou shalt not be forgotten of me.

—ISAIAH 44:21

God has not forgotten you! That is why you are reading this book today. Blood flowed from the wounds on His head to prove to you that He will always remember you. He is ever mindful of you. Amen.

Chapter 3
WOUNDS ON HIS MOUTH AND EARS

*And when he had thus spoken, one of the officers which stood by struck
Jesus with the palm of his hand, saying, Answerest thou the high priest so?*
—JOHN 18:22

*And some of them began to spit on Him and to blindfold Him
and to strike Him with their fists, saying to Him, Prophesy! And
the guards received Him with blows and by slapping Him.*
—MARK 14:65, AMP

THE GUARDS THAT slapped Jesus were not ordinary people. They were very strong soldiers whose primary responsibility was to protect their superiors from any physical attack. Their blows would be powerful and capable of causing severe injuries. From Mark 14:65, we know that there was not just one guard but several guards striking Jesus.

In John 18:22, we know that the guard who slapped Jesus thought His response to the high priest was rude. In Mark 14:65, the guards were mocking Jesus, asking Him to prophesy. In both cases, Jesus was receiving severe blows, which were causing serious injury.

Prophet Micah in his book has said, "They will strike

Israel's ruler on the cheek with a rod" (Mic. 5:1, NIV). I believe when the Roman soldiers hit Jesus on His head with the rod, a few of the blows would have landed on the cheeks of our Lord.

When we read the biblical account of this incident, we really don't get a feel of what Jesus actually went through or the reason behind it. As I have explained earlier, throughout this entire ordeal the devil used humans to execute his plan of attack against the life of Jesus. But why did they slap Jesus?

THE DEVIL WANTED TO MAKE HIM DEAF AND DUMB

Several years ago a woman came to me for prayer. She told me that her husband was a doctor who was highly educated and earning lots of money. He was well respected in his field and in society, but he was also addicted to alcohol.

One day he came home late from a party and was outside shouting and banging on the door. When she opened the door and saw his condition she became very upset. She asked her husband, "Why did you drink like this? What will people say about our family? Why don't you stop drinking?" While she was still speaking, her husband lost control of himself and slapped her across the face, knocking her to the floor.

When she got up she discovered that she was bleeding from the mouth and ear. She could not talk because of the pain and swelling in her mouth. Moments later she realized that she could not hear. Examination by a doctor revealed that her eardrum was damaged. She came to me for prayer for her hearing to be restored.

While I was playing field hockey, I remember one match when I was struck on the face by an opponent's stick. This produced a deep cut in my mouth and damaged several teeth. I was unable to talk until the pain and swelling subsided.

Any type of injury on the face can make a person deaf and dumb. And if one slap or a hit by a hockey stick could cause such serious injuries as these, imagine the damage the guards must have inflicted on Jesus' mouth and ears.

Scripture says:

> And it came to pass in process of time, that the king of Egypt died: and the children of Israel sighed by reason of the bondage, and they cried, and their cry came up unto God by reason of the bondage. And God heard their groaning, and God remembered his covenant with Abraham, with Isaac, and with Jacob.
>
> —EXODUS 2:23–24

When the Israelites were under the bondage of the Egyptian taskmasters, God heard their cries. This led to His appearance to Moses at the burning bush.

> And the LORD said, I have surely seen the affliction of my people which are in Egypt, and have heard their cry by reason of their taskmasters; for I know their sorrows.
>
> —EXODUS 3:7

God not only heard the cries of His people but also promised to deliver them.

> And I am come down to deliver them out of the hand of the Egyptians, and to bring them up out of that land unto a good land and a large, unto a land flowing with milk and honey…
>
> —EXODUS 3:8

The Bible says that when King Hezekiah was sick and was about to die he prayed to the Lord. God sent the prophet Isaiah to him saying, "Go, and say to Hezekiah, Thus saith the LORD, the God of David thy father, I have heard thy prayer, I have seen thy tears: behold, I will add unto thy days fifteen years." God even confirmed His promise to Hezekiah by turning the shadow on the sundial back ten degrees (Isa. 38:1-8).

On His way to Jerusalem, Jesus passed through Samaria and Galilee. Upon entering a certain village, ten lepers met him. The Bible says, "And they lifted up their voices, and said, Jesus, Master, have mercy on us" (Luke 17:13). Jesus heard their cries because the next verse says, "And when he saw them, he said unto them, Go shew yourselves unto the priests. And it came to pass, that, as they went, they were cleansed" (Luke 17:14).

One day, blind Bartimaeus was sitting by the road begging.

> And when he heard that it was Jesus of Nazareth, he began to cry out, and say, Jesus, thou Son of David, have mercy on me. And many charged him that he should hold his peace: but he cried the more a great deal, Thou Son of David, have mercy on me.
>
> —MARK 10:47–48

Jesus heard the cry of Bartimaeus. The Bible says:

> And Jesus stood still, and commanded him to be called. And they call the blind man, saying unto him, Be of good comfort, rise; he calleth thee. And he, casting away his garment, rose, and came to Jesus.
>
> —MARK 10:49–50

And Jesus answered and said unto him, What wilt thou that I should do unto thee? The blind man said unto him, Lord, that I might receive my sight. And Jesus said unto him, Go thy way; thy faith hath made thee whole. And immediately he received his sight, and followed Jesus in the way.

—MARK 10:51–52

Our God is a prayer-answering God. Psalm 65:2 says, "O thou that hearest prayer, unto thee shall all flesh come." He not only hears our cries but also responds to them.

Behold, the LORD's hand is not shortened, that it cannot save; neither his ear heavy, that it cannot hear.

—ISAIAH 59:1

He that planted the ear, shall he not hear? He that formed the eye, shall he not see?

—PSALM 94:9

I believe that when the guards slapped and struck Jesus on His face, the blows would have inflicted serious injuries, causing blood to flow from His mouth and ears.

The devil expected these blows to make Jesus deaf and no longer be able to hear and answer prayer. Satan's intention was to prove that God does not hear and respond to the cries of His children.

In Matthew 27:13–14, Pilate asked Jesus, "Do you not hear how many things they testify against you? But He answered him not one word, so that the governor marveled greatly" (NKJV). At this point the devil was probably thinking that he had succeeded and that Jesus was no longer a prayer-answering God.

But the Bible says that when one of the thieves who was

crucified by the side of Jesus cried out, "Lord, remember me when thou comest into thy kingdom," Jesus replied, "Verily I say unto thee, To day shalt thou be with me in paradise" (Luke 23:43).

In spite of the injuries to His mouth and ears, Jesus heard and answered the man's prayer, thwarting the plan of the devil. Hallelujah!

I remember the incident in 1987 in which a bus knocked down my father while he was riding a motorcycle. The impact was so severe that it broke the helmet he was wearing. He was immediately taken to the hospital where a medical scan revealed that he had a serious head injury, a fractured backbone, and a fractured upper right arm. In addition to this they discovered that he had had a heart attack and was suffering from high blood sugar and a urinary tract infection. His blood pressure rose to 210/170.

Several medical specialists attended on my father, but they soon lost hope due to his critical condition. The chief doctor of that hospital told me that my father was about to die. He added that even if he survived he would remain bedridden because of his fractured backbone. In fact, the doctor asked me to inform all my family members and prepare for the funeral.

To top it all, my father's accident took place just three months after my wedding. In some parts of India people are superstitious. They believe that if someone in the family passes away soon after a marriage, the bride or groom has somehow brought bad luck to the family. Of course I married my wife after much fasting and prayer and with clear guidance from God that she was the one chosen for me. But I did not want my new bride to be blamed for what was happening.

That night I went home and I cried out to our Lord Jesus

Christ. I was desperate for a miracle. I prayed fervently asking God to give life to my father. Medically, we saw only a dead man, but I knew in my heart that our Lord, the giver of life, would hear my prayers.

The next morning, a medical graduate, who was a born-again Christian, came to the room to comfort us. To our surprise my father suddenly opened his eyes and motioned to the intern to remove the oxygen mask from his face. He removed the mask thinking that my father wanted to say a few words before he died.

But as my father, who was now breathing normally, tried to get out of the bed, the intern realized that something had happened to him, so he helped my father to sit and asked him, "Are you all right?" My father nodded his head "yes."

The intern immediately called the head doctor and told him to come quickly as something miraculous had taken place in my father. After his initial examination, the head doctor took my father to a separate room for a thorough examination. Within a few moments all the medical specialists, who had attended on my father, were there examining him.

A short time later one of the doctors, a non-Christian, came out and handed me my father's medical records saying, "You should show this to an atheist because no science could prove this." He said, "The God whom you worship has answered your prayers and miraculously healed your father."

With the exception of slightly high blood pressure, my father was completely healed, and he began to walk the same day. In fact, the doctors, who did not set the broken bone in his arm and place it in a plaster cast because his condition was so critical, found that even this fracture was totally healed.

My father was healed because God heard and answered my prayer. And if God could hear my prayer in the desperate situation I was facing, then He can also hear your prayer. For we know that God is no respecter of persons (Acts 10:34; Rom. 2:11).

Isaiah 59:2 says:

> But your iniquities have separated between you and your God, and your sins have hid his face from you, that he will not hear.

The blood, which flowed from the wounds, intended by the devil to make Him deaf and hence unable to answer prayers, is the same blood that washes away your sins, the sins that separate you from God. But because of what Jesus endured, you are no longer separated from God. You can be sure that He will hear and answer your prayers.

Psalm 34:15 says, "His ears are attentive to their cry" (NIV). So cry unto him; He is a prayer-answering God, and He will surely answer. You, too, can come out of your bondage, trouble, and sickness.

THE DEVIL WANTED TO PREVENT US FROM HEARING THE VOICE OF GOD

There is another blessing available for us to receive from the wounds inflicted on His mouth and ears. From the Scriptures we know that God called the family of Aaron to the office of priest for the Israelites. The ceremony to consecrate Aaron and his sons to set them apart for the priesthood was an elaborate process. You can read about this in the Bible starting with Leviticus 8:1.

During one part of the process Aaron and his sons laid

their hands on the head of the ram of consecration as Moses killed it. Moses then took some of its blood and put it on the tip of Aaron's right ear, on the thumb of the right hand and on the big toe of his right foot. He did the same to Aaron's sons (Lev. 8:22–24).

Why did Moses do this, particularly to the right ear? We know that the priest stood in the presence of God to intercede for the people and received the word of God for the people. I believe the reason Moses applied the blood to the right ear of Aaron and his sons was to anoint them to be able to hear the Word of the Lord.

It is as if they would hear the voice of the people with one ear and hear the voice of God with the other ear. Our God is holy, and unless your ears are tuned (made holy), you cannot hear His voice. That is why Jesus' blood, which is the atonement of sin, was to be applied in the right ear.

In this case it was the blood of a ram that was applied to the ears of the priest. But Jesus, a priest forever after the order of Melchizedek, shed His blood (including blood from the wounds on his ears) to cleanse us and enable us to receive God's Word.

Revelation 1:5–6 says:

> And from Jesus Christ, who is the faithful witness, and the first begotten of the dead, and the prince of the kings of the earth. Unto him that loved us, and washed us from our sins in his own blood, And hath made us kings and priests unto God and his Father; to him be glory and dominion for ever and ever. Amen.

Therefore, you too are a priest and can hear the voice of God. Remember what Jesus said to Satan in Matthew 4:4: "It is written, Man shall not live by bread alone, but by every word that proceedeth out of the mouth of God." If you can hear and receive His Word, it will bring life, abundant life.

Since 1992 I was actively involved only in part-time ministry, as I had a full-time job. Even though I was excited about ministry, I did not wish to quit my job hastily and enter full-time ministry. In fact, I had spent a considerable amount of time praying and asking God for a clear direction.

Then one night in 2002 as I was fast asleep, I felt someone tap on my leg to wake me up. As I opened my eyes I heard a voice saying, "Son, resign your job in March 2002." These words were very clear to me, and it was a gentle command given with love. After hearing this, I resigned my job and entered full-time ministry. Since then I have been continually amazed at how God is blessing me not only in my personal life, but also in my ministry.

Our God is a living God who always speaks, and you, too, can hear His voice. Isaiah 50:4–6 (NKJV) says:

> The Lord God has given Me the tongue of the learned, That I should know how to speak a word in season to him who is weary. He awakens me morning by morning, He awakens my ear to hear as the learned. The Lord God has opened My ear; And I was not rebellious, Nor did I turn away. I gave My back to those who struck Me, And My cheeks to those who plucked out the beard; I did not hide My face from shame and spitting.

Through His suffering and the blood He shed from the wounds on His mouth and ears, Jesus has made a way for us to communicate with the one true living God.

So do not believe the lies of the devil. God always hears and answers your prayers. He is with you all the time. You can hear His voice and speak to the living God. It is all because of His blood, which was shed from His mouth and ears. Thank you, Lord, for Your precious blood!

Chapter 4
WOUNDS ON HIS EYES

*And some of them began to spit on Him and to blindfold Him
And to strike Him with their fists, saying to Him, Prophesy! And
the guards received Him with blows and by slapping Him.*

—MARK 14:65, AMP

*As many were astonished at him—his appearance was so marred, beyond
human semblance, and his form beyond that of the sons of men.*

—ISAIAH 52:14, RSV

HAVE YOU BEEN to a boxing match? In the name of sport, two men strap on leather gloves and punch each other. Points are awarded for the number and accuracy of the blows. Delivering punches to the face and head is rated highly.

The object of the match, of course, is to outscore your opponent. But an alternative way to win is to strike your opponent hard several times so that he falls down and is unable to get up. This is called a knock-out.

The competition is brutal and sometimes the boxers will end up with cuts around their eyes and mouth. Their faces will be bruised and their eyes swollen shut. And this decides the winners. The losers are sometimes beaten beyond recognition and, because of their injuries, are horrific to look at.

The blows that the Roman soldiers delivered to the face of Jesus, either with their fists or with the reed, caused injuries like these, including His eyes being swollen shut. It is likely that the sharp thorns in the crown penetrated the skin around His eyes. In addition to this, some of the blood and perspiration running down His forehead would have entered His eyes. All of this would have made it very difficult for Jesus to see.

Back in chapter 2, I told you how my father was unable to recognize my mother during the medical examination following his head injury. My father later explained the reason for this. He said that he had previously lost most of the sight in his left eye and directly above his right eye was the cut he received during his fall down the steps. The injury caused the eyebrow and eyelid to swell making it difficult for him to see. In addition to this, there was blood and fluid oozing from the wound and running down into his eye. All of this made it impossible for him to recognize my mother.

If my father could not see properly due to the injury to his eyebrow, imagine how difficult it must have been for our Lord to see following the wounds He endured. So why were His eyebrows and eyelids hurt like this?

We know that when people are in trouble and facing challenges, God sees them and is able to respond.

For example, there was Hagar, Sarai's maid. Sarai was unable to conceive and gave Hagar to her husband Abram as a wife, in order that she might obtain children by her. But when Hagar conceived, she started despising her mistress. Because of this, Sarai dealt with her harshly, forcing Hagar to flee into the wilderness (Gen. 16:1–6).

Even though Hagar was wandering in the wilderness, God saw her and led her back to her mistress with a wonderful promise. "And she called the name of the Lord that spake unto her, Thou God sees me: for she said, Have I also here looked after him that see me?" (Gen. 16:13). God sees His children and gives them *deliverance*.

Then there was Noah. Genesis 6:8 says, "But Noah found grace in the eyes of the LORD." As a result, God instructed Noah to build an ark in which his family was saved from the great flood. God sees His children and gives them *grace*.

Zechariah 2:8 contains a prophecy about the church and its glory and protection through the presence of God in it. "For thus saith the LORD of hosts; After the glory hath he sent me unto the nations which spoiled you: for he that toucheth you toucheth the apple of his eye." God sees them and gives *protection*.

The following Scripture clearly confirms the fact that when God sees a person He delivers him, He instructs him, and He protects him.

"He found him in a desert land, and in the waste howling wilderness; he led him about, he *instructed* him, he kept him as *the apple of his eye*" (Deut. 32:10, emphasis added).

When a man sees a person, he may look upon the man or woman with envy and jealousy. When the devil sees a person it is with an evil eye. But when God sees a person, the person receives blessings. This is the character of God, which is also reflected in Jesus Christ before and after the wounds inflicted on His eyes.

Before His crucifixion, Jesus entered the city of Nain and came upon a funeral procession. The dead man was the only son of a widow. The Bible says that when Jesus saw her, He had compassion on her. She did not call out to Jesus, but He saw her.

Jesus touched the coffin and stopped the funeral procession. He said, "Young man, I say unto thee, Arise." The young man sat up and began to speak as Jesus presented him to his mother (Luke 7:11–15). Jesus delivered the man from death and led him back to his mother.

One day Jesus was teaching in the temple. The Scribes and Pharisees brought to Him a woman caught in adultery. They told Him that the law demanded that such a person be stoned. They wanted to see what Jesus would do in this situation so that they could accuse Him. But Jesus stooped down and began to write on the ground with His finger. When they persisted, He stood up and said to them, "He that is without sin among you, let him first cast a stone at her." And again He stooped down and wrote on the ground. One by one they departed until there was no one remaining except the woman. Jesus said to her, "Woman, where are those thine accusers? hath no man condemned thee? She said, No man, Lord. And Jesus said unto her, Neither do I condemn thee: go, and sin no more" (John 8:3–11). Jesus had every right to throw the first stone, but instead He showed her grace and forgave her sins and instructed her to go and sin no more.

Here the eyes of the scribes and Pharisees were evil toward the adulterous lady and toward Jesus. But the eyes of the Lord brought grace, forgiveness, and instruction.

Just prior to His betrayal and arrest in Gethsemane, Jesus prayed for the protection of His disciples. "I pray not that thou shouldest take them out of the world, but that thou shouldest keep them from the evil" (John 17:15).

When the soldiers came to arrest Him, Jesus was still protecting His disciples. In John 18:7–8 Jesus asked them again, "Whom seek ye? And they said, Jesus of Nazareth. Jesus answered, I have told you that I am he: if therefore ye seek me, let these go their way."

Even during His arrest, when Jesus saw that the soldiers of the high priest were also arresting His disciples, He gave His disciples protection. When Jesus saw the crying widow He brought deliverance. When He saw the woman caught in adultery He brought forgiveness, grace, and instruction.

Satan also knows the Scriptures. That is why he tried so hard to inflict injuries on Jesus that would prevent Him from being able to see. But in spite of the swelling and bleeding from the wounds around His eyes, Jesus was still able to see, deliver, instruct, and protect.

Despite the wounds, Jesus was able to see the soldiers and Jewish leaders responsible for His suffering and death and give them grace and forgiveness. "Then said Jesus, Father, forgive them; for they know not what they do. And they parted his raiment, and cast lots" (Luke 23:34).

Not only were His murderers spared because Jesus offered this prayer but also the entire human race. This prayer of Jesus has brought deliverance to us all.

Even with His eyes wounded, Jesus was able to see the multitude and the women who followed Him on the way to the cross and to instruct them.

> And there followed him a great company of people, and of women, which also bewailed and lamented him. But Jesus turning unto them said: Daughters of Jerusalem, weep not for me, but weep for yourselves, and for your children. For, behold, the days are coming, in the which they shall say, Blessed are the barren, and the wombs that never bare, and the paps which never gave suck. Then shall they begin to say to the mountains,

Fall on us; and to the hills, Cover us. For if they do
these things in a green tree, what shall be done in the
dry?

—LUKE 23:27–31

Jesus was able to see His mother and disciple and give
instructions for the care and protection of His mother.

When Jesus therefore saw his mother, and the disciple
standing by, whom he loved, he saith unto his mother,
Woman, behold thy son! Then saith he to the disciple,
Behold thy mother! And from that hour that disciple
took her unto his own home.

—JOHN 19:26–27

Jesus defeated the devil's plan and proved that He is the
God who sees the afflictions of His people. "He that planted
the ear, shall he not hear? He that formed the eye, shall he not
see?" (Ps. 94:9). The blood that Jesus shed from the wounds
to His eyes will deliver you, instruct you, and keep you as the
apple of His eye.

I still remember the day in October 1992 when the pastor
of the small English-speaking congregation that I was
attending asked me to pray for the offering. When I stepped
up to the pulpit and took the microphone, my entire body
began to shake. I was so afraid to speak in public that words
would not come out of my mouth. I blabbered something,
put the microphone down, and rushed back to my seat.

Then the pastor came forward and took the microphone
saying, "Shall we all close our eyes and pray for the offering."
This gives you an idea of the kind of prayer I must have
offered that made it necessary for the pastor to pray again!

I was so embarrassed that after the service I quietly slipped away and I did not go to that church for many months.

A few months later, early in the morning of December 14, I was praying with my eyes closed and suddenly felt something like a warm light illuminating me. At first I thought my wife had entered the room and switched on the light. But when I opened my eyes I saw a wide, oval-shaped light in front of me and standing in the midst of the light was our Lord Jesus.

He just looked at me and though He did not speak audibly, I understood from His countenance that He was telling me, "Son, I have molded you for twelve years; come and do My ministry." I immediately responded in my mind, "Lord I will support your ministry." Again He looked at me and I knew what He was saying. He said, "I don't want your money; I want *you.*"

I told the Lord, "You know what happened to me that day in the English-speaking church. I'm not an orator, I suffer from stage fright. I cannot speak in public because I am so much afraid." Then He said, "I will make you speak." I could not argue with God and finally I told Him that if it was His will for me to preach His Word, I would surrender my life to Him. He smiled and immediately I felt a power had descended upon me, and from that point on I had the confidence that I can do something big for God.

The Lord, who sees me, has delivered me from stage fright, continues to give me instructions, and is protecting me. The very look from His eyes has given me the power to do ministry.

Second Chronicles 16:9 says, "For the eyes of the LORD run to and fro throughout the whole earth, to shew himself strong in the behalf of them whose heart is perfect toward him. Herein thou hast done foolishly: therefore from hence-forth thou shalt have wars." He is the God who is always looking for a person to show His might.

Psalm 121:1–2 (NKJV) says:

> I will lift up my eyes to the hills—From whence comes my help? My help comes from the LORD, Who made heaven and earth.

When you lift your eyes to the King of kings He will certainly deliver, instruct, and protect you. The blood that He shed from His eyes has the power to bring all these bless-ings in your life.

Chapter 5
WOUNDS ON HIS FACE

As many were astonied at thee; his visage was so marred more
than any man, and his form more than the sons of men.

—ISAIAH 52:14

THE ROMAN GUARDS who were given the responsibility of scourging Jesus were proficient at their
work. They hit and struck Him with their fists.
They flogged Him with a whip and beat Him with a rod. The
Roman soldiers also hit Jesus with the rod (Mic. 5:1). They
humiliated Him by spitting on His face and mocked Him by
placing a crown of thorns on His head.

These things alone were enough to cause severe injuries
to the face of Jesus. However, it is possible that the crown of
thorns would have also pierced His forehead and eyebrows,
causing more bleeding and swelling. And the guard flogging
Him might not have always struck accurately, thus allowing
the whip to strike Jesus in the face also.

Referring to Jesus, Isaiah 50:6 says, "I gave my back to the
smiters, and my cheeks to them that plucked off the hair: I
hid not my face from shame and spitting." From this scripture it seems that His beard was plucked and removed. All
of this was not only painful but would have left the face of
Jesus marred, disfigured, and perhaps even unrecognizable.

"As people were surprised at him, And his face was not beautiful, so as to be desired…" (Isaiah 52:14, BBE).

The prophet Isaiah was given a glimpse of the brutal suffering that Jesus would undergo. His vision is recorded in the Bible in the book of Isaiah.

> Who hath believed our report? And to whom is the arm of the LORD revealed? For he shall grow up before him as a tender plant, and as a root out of a dry ground: he hath no form nor comeliness; and when we shall see him, there is no beauty that we should desire him. He is despised and rejected of men; a man of sorrows, and acquainted with grief: and we hid as it were our faces from him; he was despised, and we esteemed him not. Surely he hath borne our griefs, and carried our sorrows: yet we did esteem him stricken, smitten of God, and afflicted. But he was wounded for our transgressions, he was bruised for our iniquities: the chastisement of our peace was upon him; and with his stripes we are healed.
>
> —ISAIAH 53:1–5

Verse 2 says that when we see Him, "there is no beauty that we should desire him." People love to see a beautiful face, and everyone has some trait of beauty. Look close enough at anyone and you will discover something to admire. But the Bible says there is no beauty in Him that we should desire Him. Not one part of His face or body was beautiful because they were so marred and disfigured by His wounds.

Normally when there has been an accident, people would avoid looking at the victim. They are not interested in seeing a marred or disfigured body. After my seventy-five-year-old father fell down the steps, we lifted him up and discovered that he was bleeding from his head, his face was bruised, and his lips were swollen. His entire face had changed and he looked ghastly.

If my father's bruised and blood-stained face was so horrible and difficult to look at, just imagine what the face of Jesus must have looked like. The Scripture says that the face of Jesus was so marred that we would have hidden our faces from Him (Isa. 53:3).

Of all the pictures and paintings I have seen depicting Jesus, none of them shows a marred or disfigured face. Christians are not interested in displaying the mutilated face of Jesus in their homes or in public. The fact is His face was marred and disfigured, but no one wants to visualize this sort of thing.

WHY WAS HIS FACE SO MUTILATED?

Throughout the Bible there are references to Jesus being a bridegroom and the church His bride. (Isa. 62:5; Rev. 19:7). The beauty of the bridegroom is described in Song of Solomon 5:10–16:

> My beloved is white and ruddy, the chiefest among ten thousand. His head is as the most fine gold, his locks are bushy, and black as a raven. His eyes are as the eyes of doves by the rivers of waters, washed with milk, and fitly set. His cheeks are as a bed of spices, as sweet flowers: his lips like lilies, dropping sweet smelling myrrh. His hands are as gold rings set with the beryl: his belly is as bright ivory overlaid with sapphires. His legs are as pillars of marble, set upon sockets of fine gold: his countenance is as Lebanon, excellent as the cedars. His mouth is most sweet: yea, he is altogether

lovely. This is my beloved, and this is my friend, O daughters of Jerusalem.

Finally in verse 16, the writer concludes that He (the bridegroom) is altogether lovely. Here Jesus is described as being beautiful, made in perfection, pure, undefiled, someone that we would like to see and admire.

Zacchaeus wanted to see Jesus. "And he ran before, and climbed up into a sycamore tree to see him: for he was to pass that way. And when Jesus came to the place, he looked up, and saw him, and said unto him, Zacchaeus, make haste, and come down; for today I must abide at thy house." When Zacchaeus saw Jesus, salvation came to him and his entire family (Luke 19:4–10).

Nathanael wanted to see Jesus. At first he asked, "Can there any good thing come out of Nazareth?" After seeing Jesus he declared, "Rabbi, thou art the Son of God; thou art the King of Israel" (John 1:46–49).

The Bible tells us that God spoke to Moses face to face (Num. 12:8). When Moses came down from Mount Sinai after his encounter with God, his face was shining and the people could not see it (Exod. 34:30–35).

Psalm 34:5 says, "They looked unto him, and were lightened: and their faces were not ashamed." Those who look unto God and seek His face will be lightened or illuminated.

For example, to polish shoes we first remove the dirt and then apply the wax. Next we buff the shoes until they have a lustrous shine. In the same way the blood that Jesus shed from the wounds on His face removes the dirt (sin) from our lives and polishes (lightens) our countenance.

The Lord make his face shine upon thee, and be gracious unto thee.

—NUMBERS 6:25

The devil knows these things too. He wants people to remain in darkness and have no desire to seek the face of Jesus. He knows that those who seek the face of Jesus will see Him and be lightened and will never be put to shame. That is why Satan had the guards and the soldiers mutilate the face of Jesus.

Yes, the face of our Lord Jesus was indeed marred and disfigured. But one of the thieves hanging on a cross next to Jesus looked upon that mutilated face. He was changed forever and went on to paradise along with Jesus (Luke 23:42–43).

Then there was the Roman centurion. He had witnessed the crucifixion of many men but none had an effect on him like the crucifixion of Jesus. He looked upon the disfigured face of Jesus and declared, "Truly this was the Son of God" (Matt. 27:54).

Those who saw the mutilated face did receive their salvation. Their lives were changed, they were lightened, and they were not put to shame.

A man named Saul was on his way to Damascus to persecute Christians. When he saw Jesus, his life was changed and so was his name (Acts 9:3–6). He was known as the apostle Paul, full of the Holy Spirit, who went on to write much of the New Testament and literally shook the world.

In India a man named Sadhu Sundar Singh was against Christians. He was desperate to see the face of the true God. One day in despair he cried out saying he would end his life if the true God did not reveal Himself to him. Suddenly Jesus

45

appeared to him and, like the apostle Paul, Sadhu Sundar Singh spent the rest of his life serving the Lord.

In my life I had often heard testimonies of people who claimed that they had seen the face of Jesus. For a long time I wondered if that would ever happen to me.

In 1980 I left my hometown and moved to the city of Madras, which is now called Chennai. I suddenly found myself alone in new surroundings and I did not like it. For the sake of my new job and sports career I decided to stay there. After a while I felt lonely and started to feel spiritual oppression from the powers of darkness.

So I began to cry out to the Lord saying, "Lord, are you with me? Lord, do you love me? Lord, I want to see you!" Suddenly one day as I was praying like this I saw a vision. In the vision was Jesus, who was standing at an angle away from me. Slowly Jesus began to turn towards me until He was looking directly at me. As soon as I saw His face, He smiled at me and then disappeared. Immediately I felt the spiritual oppression leave me.

When I came out of my prayer room, my mother who came to see me looked at me and asked, "What happened to you? Your face is shining." This encounter with Jesus brought about light inside me.

Are you living in darkness? Do you feel spiritual oppression? Do you need deliverance? Do you want light in your life? Then look upon the mutilated face of Jesus Christ.

Isaiah 50:7 (NKJV) says, "For the Lord God will help Me; Therefore I will not be disgraced; Therefore I have set My face like a flint, And I know that I will not be ashamed."

This verse tells us that Jesus made His face like flint, meaning that He was determined to bring blessings into our lives. The blood that was shed from the wounds on the face of Jesus has the power to lighten your life, and you will not be put to shame.

Therefore, "Arise, shine; For your light has come! And the glory of the Lord is risen upon you. For behold, the darkness shall cover the earth, And deep darkness the people; But the Lord will arise over you, And His glory will be seen upon you. The Gentiles shall come to your light, And kings to the brightness of your rising" (Isa. 60:1–3, NKJV).

Chapter 6
SPIT ON HIS FACE

Then did they spit in his face, and buffeted him; and
others smote him with the palms of their hands.
—MATTHEW 26:67

And they spit upon him, and took the reed, and smote him on the head.
—MATTHEW 27:30

FROM THE ABOVE Scriptures we can see that the heathen Roman soldiers, as well as the Jews, who were Jesus' own people and the seeds of Abraham, spat on the face of Jesus.

In the first incident, the Jewish high priest adjured Jesus by the living God to tell them whether or not He was the Christ, the Son of God. Without hesitation, Jesus replied, "Thou hast said: nevertheless I say unto you, hereafter shall ye see the Son of man sitting on the right hand of power, and coming in the clouds of heaven" (Matt. 26:63–64).

Jesus' answer infuriated the high priest, the elders, and all the council members. They considered it blasphemy for Jesus to declare that He was the Son of God. They concluded that He deserved the death penalty.

After the high priest pronounced judgment, the Bible says,

"Then did they spit in his face..." (Matt. 26:67). From this response, we can conclude that the act of spitting on the face of Jesus showed their approval of the verdict and indicated their agreement with His condemnation.

In the second incident, the Roman soldiers, who put the crown of thorns on Jesus' head, also spat on His face. They spat on Jesus to mock Him because he had called himself the King of Jews (Matt. 27:30).

From these two instances we derive that the act of spitting on Jesus was not only an angry reaction, but also an act of condemnation and mockery.

SPITTING IS AN ACT OF ANGER

When we carefully study the Scripture, we can see that Jesus Himself had foretold that His enemies would spit on His face.

> Behold, we are going up to Jerusalem, and the Son of Man will be betrayed to the chief priests and to the scribes; and they will condemn Him to death and deliver Him to the Gentiles; and they will mock Him, and scourge Him, and *spit on Him*, and kill Him. And the third day He will rise again.
> —MARK 10:33–34, NKJV, EMPHASIS ADDED

Also, the prophet Isaiah predicted that the Son of God would be spat upon. Isaiah 50:6 says, "I gave My back to the smiters, and My cheeks to them that plucked off the hair: I hid not My face from shame and spitting."

These were not just random acts of anger. When they spat on the face of Jesus, it was the fulfillment of the prophecies. But there are other reasons why the Son of God had to endure such a humiliating punishment.

When He stood before Pontius Pilate, Jesus made it very clear that unless power was given from above, Pilate had no authority over Him (John 19:11). In other words, nothing could happen to Jesus unless the Almighty God had permitted it.

But God allowed every wound, every punishment, every suffering, and every act of humiliation inflicted on Jesus, so that Jesus could carry our sorrows and take the punishment that we deserve.

> Surely He hath borne our griefs, and carried our sorrows: yet we did esteem him stricken, smitten of God, and afflicted. But he was wounded for our transgressions, he was bruised for our iniquities: the chastisement of our peace was upon him; and with his stripes we are healed.
>
> —ISAIAH 53:4–5

Therefore, spitting on the face of Jesus was more than just a simple reaction by the people. Let us look into the hidden reasons why Jesus endured the spitting on His face.

GOD OF COMPASSION

Numerous Scripture verses throughout the Bible describe our God as being full of compassion, long-suffering, and so on.

> And the LORD passed by before him, and proclaimed, the LORD, the LORD God, merciful and gracious, long-suffering, and abundant in goodness and truth.
>
> —EXODUS 34:6

But thou, O Lord, art a God full of compassion, and gracious, long suffering and plenteous in mercy and truth.

—PSALM 86:15

And it shall come to pass, after that I have plucked them out I will return, and have compassion on them, and will bring them again, every man to his heritage, and every man to his land.

—JEREMIAH 12:15

The Lord is not slack concerning his promise, as some men count slackness; but is long-suffering to us-ward, not willing that any should perish, but that all should come to repentance.

—2 PETER 3:9

That is the reason why the Bible describes Him as slow to anger. For example:

The LORD is merciful and gracious, slow to anger, and plenteous in mercy.

—PSALM 103:8

The LORD is gracious, and full of compassion; slow to anger, and of great mercy.

—PSALM 145:8

And he prayed unto the LORD, and said, I pray thee, O LORD, was not this my saying, when I was yet in my country? Therefore I fled before unto Tarshish: for I knew that thou art a gracious God, and merciful, slow to anger, and of great kindness, and repentest thee of the evil.

—JONAH 4:2

HE TOO CAN GET PROVOKED

But we need to understand that even though He is patient, longsuffering, and slow to anger, He still gets angry. We can see from the Scripture there were times when people did evil things that provoked God to anger.

During the time of Noah, the Bible says, "And God saw that the wickedness of man was great in the earth, and that every imagination of the thoughts of his heart was only evil continually" (Gen. 6:5). "And God said unto Noah, The end of all flesh is come before me; for the earth is filled with violence through them; and, behold, I will destroy them with the earth" (Gen. 6:13).

God sent two angels to destroy Sodom and Gomorrah because of the depravity that existed there. They warned Lot, "For we will destroy this place, because the cry of them is waxen great before the face of the LORD; and the LORD hath sent us to destroy it" (Gen. 19:13). "Then the LORD rained upon Sodom and upon Gomorrah brimstone and fire from the LORD out of heaven" (Gen. 19:24).

When provoked to anger, God brought death and destruction to the earth and its inhabitants. That is why the Bible says, "Kiss the Son, lest He be angry, and ye perish from the way, when his wrath is kindled but a little. Blessed are all they that put their trust in him" (Ps. 2:12).

Let us look at yet another example of God's reaction when provoked to anger.

In Numbers 12:1–14, Miriam and Aaron were critical of their brother Moses and spoke against him because he had married an Ethiopian woman. They said, "Hath the LORD indeed spoken only by Moses? Hath he not spoken also by us? And the LORD heard it" (Num. 12:2).

Then the Lord called Moses, Miriam, and Aaron and came down in a pillar of cloud to meet them at the door of the tabernacle. He rebuked Miriam and Aaron for speaking against Moses, His servant. Numbers 12:9 says, "And the anger of the LORD was kindled against them; and he departed."

As soon as the cloud departed from above the tabernacle, Miriam became leprous, as white as snow. When Aaron saw her, he pleaded with Moses and repented for their foolish actions. Moses cried out to the Lord, praying for God to heal Miriam.

Then the Lord said to Moses, "If her father had but spit in her face, should she not be ashamed seven days? Let her be shut out from the camp seven days, and after that let her be received in again" (Num. 12:14).

What did God do here? If Miriam's earthly father had spat in her face, it would have been a token of His anger and displeasure, meant to shame and disgrace her. It would have made her unclean and required her to be kept apart, separated for seven days.

It was as though God, her heavenly Father, had spat on Miriam. Here spittle can be likened to leprosy. Leprosy came about from the mouth of the Lord, so to speak, by His order, just as spittle from a man.

Clearly, God was angry and displeased with Miriam for speaking out against Moses, His servant and chosen vessel. The Scripture says that this is the reason the heavenly Father forced her to live outside the camp for seven days. We can see that spitting is yet another response of God when provoked to anger.

Spitting Is an Act of Condemnation

In the Old Testament, God established a law stating that if brothers dwell together and one of them dies without a son, the surviving brother must take his brother's widow as a wife. He must perform the duty of a husband's brother and the first-born son, which she bears, will succeed the name of his dead brother (Deut. 25:5–6).

This was God's method of preserving a family line and the reason why we are able to trace the genealogy of Jesus all the way back to Adam (Luke 3:23–37). So when the surviving brother refused to perform his duty, it was a serious matter and had to be dealt with harshly.

If the man does not take his brother's wife, "Then shall his brother's wife come unto him in the presence of the elders, and loose his shoe from off his foot, and spit in his face, and shall answer and say, so shall it be done unto that man that will not build up his brother's house" (Deut. 25:9). Here we can see that spitting in the face is an act of condemnation against the man for not taking the responsibility for his deceased brother's wife.

Several years ago, one of my relatives in India fell in love with a man from a different caste and married him. Both families condemned the couple and rejected them. They literally spat on them in order to show their displeasure. But today they are a blessed and wealthy couple.

Spitting Is an Act of Mockery

There is yet another reason for spitting. We know the story of Job. Satan took his family, his wealth, and all of his possessions (Job 1:12–22). Satan was also allowed to attack his health, but not to take his life (Job 2:6).

Now that he was poor, alone, and in failing health, Job became an object of ridicule, a laughing stock to those around him. Job 30:1 says, "But now they that are younger than I have me in derision, whose fathers I would have disdained to have set with the dogs of my flock." Job said, "They abhor me, they flee far from me, and spare not to spit in my face" (Job 30:10).

Another word for *derision* is *mockery*. Sadly, when a person loses his health and wealth, people will mock him. And in this case, when they mocked Job, they also spat on his face. Here we can see that spitting is a form of mockery.

When I was studying in grade 3, a friend of mine suddenly turned against me. Whenever he saw me, he would spit on the ground to show that he did not like me. With each act of spitting, he was publicly mocking me and humiliating me. After some time, we settled our differences and became friends again.

Though years have passed and I have forgiven my friend, those acts of humiliation are still fresh in my mind. Of course spitting did not wound my physical body, but it did wound my inner person, that is, my mind and emotion. In the same way, I believe that when the Roman soldiers and the Jews spat on Jesus, it would have wounded His inner person. After all, He was then just as human as you and I.

But Jesus endured the spitting on His face in order to save us from the anger of God, to save us from condemnation, and to save us from the shame of mocking people.

We can also say that He intercedes for us before God continually by saying that He has already taken the punishment. His humiliation and suffering have brought us peace with God; it helps us escape from the curse of the law and protects us from the shame of mockery.

Spitting Is an Act of Spreading Disease

In every corner of the hospital where my father was admitted for his head injury, there was a sign board reading, "Do Not Spit." Now, this may seem strange to you, but in India it is customary for some people to chew a mild stimulant called betel nut and spit it out. It is a vicious habit that can be compared to chewing tobacco in other parts of the world.

Knowing that a person's saliva may contain viruses or bacteria, it is understandable that the hospital would want to maintain sanitary conditions to prevent the spread of infectious diseases.

Many years ago, I went to a slum area to preach the gospel. At that time there was an infection called "Madras eye" prevalent in that locality. If it infected people, their eyes would swell, so that they could not see. They would have to stay home for at least three days to recover. Sometimes it could even infect a person who just looked at an infected person. After the message, most of them who were affected by this eye infection came forward for prayer. I laid my hands on them and prayed for all of them. Praise the Lord! That infection did not affect me at all. I was able to carry on our Lord's work for all the three days I was there. In Psalm 91:10 we read, "There shall no evil befall thee, neither shall any plague come nigh thy dwelling."

Our Lord not only heals us from our sicknesses, but He also protects us from infections. In Exodus 15:26 God said, "I will put none of these diseases upon thee, which I have brought upon the Egyptians: for I am the Lord that healeth thee." The Bible says that, "By His stripes we are healed" (Isa. 53:5, NKJV). Even the humiliation and emotional wounds He suffered were for our blessing.

Blessing Through His Spit

Our Lord took the spit on His face in order to save us from the anger of God, to save us from condemnation, to save those of us who are mocked, and also to spare us from disease. At the same time, it is amazing to know that it brings healing and anointing into our lives.

When a blind man was brought to Jesus in Bethsaida, He led him out of the town and spat on his eyes, and this brought sight to that blind man (Mark 8:22–26). In the same way, for a person who was deaf and had an impediment in speech, Jesus put His finger into his ear and He spat and touched his tongue and said, "*Ephphatha*," that is, "Be opened." Immediately, the ears of this deaf man were opened, the tongue was loosened, and he spoke plainly (Mark 7: 32–35).

In the same manner, Jesus spat on the ground, made clay from His spit, anointed the eyes of a blind man with that clay, and asked him to wash in the pond of Siloam (this word means "sent"). When the blind man did exactly what Jesus said, he received his sight (John 9:6–7). In this instance, Jesus used His spit to anoint the eyes of the blind man.

Jesus' spit restored sight to the sightless and hearing to the deaf; it loosened the tongue and sent (anointed) the blind, and made him a witness to others.

These miracles will symbolically bring about the following blessings for us: It opens the spiritual eyes of a person to see the truth, enables the ear to hear His word, loosens the tongue to praise Him, and anoints the person to be empowered to do God's work.

Chapter 7
WOUNDS ON HIS BACK

Then Pilate therefore took Jesus, and scourged him.
—JOHN 19:1

*I gave my back to the smiters, and my cheeks to them that plucked
off the hair: I hid not my face from shame and spitting.*
—ISAIAH 50:6

EVERAL YEARS AGO I had the opportunity to travel to
the Holy Land where I saw a replica of the whip used
by the Roman soldiers to scourge Jesus. This whip
consisted of a short handle and several long heavy leather
straps. Embedded in each strap were pieces of metal and
bone to add weight and for greater impact. The pieces of
metal and bone also protruded from the strap long enough
to form sharp hooks.

The Roman soldiers applied the whip with full force to
the shoulders, chest, back, legs, and face of Jesus. At first the
heavy straps penetrated the skin, but as the blows continued,
they cut deeper and deeper into the flesh. Each time the whip
was drawn back to deliver another blow, the metal and bone
hooks grabbed and tore pieces of skin and flesh.

It is unlikely that the Roman soldiers would have followed

the ancient Jewish law limiting the punishment to only forty lashes. They would have continued until the back of Jesus was an unrecognizable mass of torn and bleeding flesh. When the officer in charge determined that the orders of the governor had been carried out, the beating was finally stopped.

Psalm 129:3 says:

> The plowers plowed upon my back: they made long their furrows.

This scripture describes the scourged back of Jesus as a ploughed field with long furrows. We know that when a farmer ploughs his field, the blade of the plough penetrates deep into the ground, cutting a long furrow, churning up the earth below and bringing it to the surface.

The scourging of Jesus cut long furrows on His back, churning up the flesh below and bringing it to the surface, leaving Him weak, exhausted, and unable to stand upright due to the pain of His injuries. Why did they scourge Him? Why did they plough His back?

Jesus Endured the Scourging so That We Can Stand Upright

As punishment for tempting Adam and Eve to disobey God, God pronounced a curse on the serpent: "Because thou hast done this, thou art cursed above all cattle, and above every beast of the field; upon thy belly shalt thou go, and dust shalt thou eat all the days of thy life" (Gen. 3:14). From that point forward the serpent would crawl on his belly, eating dust.

While it is unclear exactly how the serpent propelled himself before the curse, it is safe to say that it must have been upright in some manner; otherwise, God's curse would have been insignificant. Therefore, we can say that God's curse broke the back of the serpent, forcing him to crawl on the ground.

In retaliation, Satan wanted to inflict the same punishment on Jesus. He wanted to break the back of Jesus, preventing Him from standing upright and forcing Him to bend down carrying the cross.

God always wants His children to stand upright. Psalm 20:6–8 (emphasis added) says:

> Now know I that the LORD saveth his anointed; he will hear him from his holy heaven with the saving strength of his right hand. Some trust in chariots, and some in horses: but we will remember the name of the LORD our God. They are brought down and fallen: *but we are risen, and stand upright.*

Whatever your past may be, Jesus and the blood He shed from the wounds on His back will give you a new life and make you stand upright in society.

There was the woman who was bent over for eighteen years. When Jesus laid His hands on her, immediately "she was made straight, and glorified God" (Luke 13:11–13).

Psalm 145:14 says:

> The Lord upholdeth all that fall, and raiseth up all those that be bowed down.

Psalm 146:8 says:

> The Lord openeth the eyes of the blind: the Lord raiseth them that are bowed down: the Lord loveth the righteous.

There were already deep wounds in Jesus' back following the severe scourging He received at the hands of the Roman soldiers; they forced Him to carry the heavy cross. This cross was not a smooth, highly polished work of art, like what we see hanging in some churches. This cross was an instrument of suffering and death and was probably made from rough-hewed wood. Undoubtedly this would have caused additional wounds to His back.

But the blood He shed from the wounds caused by carrying the cross has made a way for Jesus to carry our burdens. He knows what it is like to be laden heavily. That is why He could say, "Come unto me, all ye that labour and are heavy laden, and I will give you rest" (Matt. 11:28). Sometimes we try to carry the weight of our problems on our backs. But just like that rugged cross, Jesus wants to carry our burdens for us.

Are you carrying the burden of sickness or pain? Are you carrying the burden of debt or financial problems? Are you feeling sad and lonely? Do you feel like you are bent with the weight of the world on your shoulders? Then cast your burdens on Jesus. Let Him remove the burden from your shoulders and help you to get back on your feet.

Isaiah 10:27 says:

> And it shall come to pass in that day, that his burden shall be taken away from off thy shoulder, and his yoke from off thy neck, and the yoke shall be destroyed because of the anointing.

I remember the story of a rich man who owned a hotel. He was an influential man who was highly respected in his city. People from miles around came to him, seeking his opinion and advice on every kind of matter.

But one day his son ran away with a servant maid who was

working in the hotel. Because of this, the man was disgraced. His reputation was ruined and he eventually lost his business. He went from a position of respect to being ridiculed and looked down upon by society.

Such disgrace is nothing new to Jesus. Even His own brothers rejected Him. "His brethren therefore said unto him, Depart hence, and go into Judea, that thy disciples also may see the works that thou doest. For there is no man that doeth anything in secret, and he himself seeketh to be known openly. If thou do these things, shew thyself to the world. For neither did his brethren believe in him" (John 7:3–5).

Since Jesus Himself underwent disgrace both before and during crucifixion, He is able to sympathize with us whenever our backs are bent down by the devil and He makes us stand upright because of the blood shed from His back.

He is the "stone which the builders rejected has become the chief cornerstone" (Ps. 118:22, NKJV). When we are in Jesus, He becomes the cornerstone that sets our lives straight.

I have heard testimonies of how some criminals found Jesus while serving their terms in the prison and turned out as great preachers. People who rejected them earlier now accept them. It is not too late to give your life to Jesus so that He can set things right and give you a new life.

The scourging and severe injuries on the back would have made it very difficult for Jesus to stand upright. I remember a friend telling me about a back injury he once had. He described how one tiny bone in his lower back shifted slightly, exerting pressure on the nerves. This pressure caused the muscles in his back to spasm and contract, twisting his upper body and bending him forward. The injury was not only painful but also left him unable to stand upright for several days.

If one tiny bone shifting slightly out of joint can cause a

problem like this, imagine how excruciating the pain must have been for Jesus.

Psalm 22:12–18 speaks about the sufferings of Jesus and parallels what is described in the gospels.

> Many bulls have compassed me: strong bulls of Bashan have beset me round. They gaped upon me with their mouths, as a ravening and a roaring lion. I am poured out like water, and all my bones are out of joint: my heart is like wax; it is melted in the midst of my bowels. My strength is dried up like a potsherd; and my tongue cleaveth to my jaws; and thou hast brought me into the dust of death.
>
> —PSALM 22:12–15

The strong bulls represent the high priest and other Jewish leaders as well as Herod, Pilate, and the Roman soldiers assigned the task of crucifying Jesus. They opened their mouths wide to mock Him, blaspheme Him, and shout, "Crucify Him, crucify Him," behaving like roaring lions that seek and greedily devour their prey.

As He endured the punishment, His life was being poured out, leaving Him unable to stand upright as though all of His bones were out of joint. His heart melted like wax as the wrath and fury of God was poured out upon Him like fire for the sins of mankind. His strength was dried up like a piece of pottery being burned in the furnace, leaving Him parched and thirsting. All of this brought Him to the verge of death.

In John 3:14 Jesus said:

> And as Moses lifted up the serpent in the wilderness, even so must the Son of man be lifted up.

He was referring to the incident in the wilderness where the Israelites spoke against God and Moses. As a result of their rebellion, "The Lord sent fiery serpents among the people, and they bit the people; and much people of Israel died" (Num. 21:6).

When they realized their sin, the people of Israel came to Moses and he prayed for them.

> And the Lord said unto Moses, Make thee a fiery serpent, and set it upon a pole: and it shall come to pass, that every one that is bitten, when he looketh upon it, shall live. And Moses made a serpent of brass, and put it upon a pole, and it came to pass, that if a serpent had bitten any man, when he beheld the serpent of brass, he lived.
>
> —NUMBERS 21:8–9

When Jesus was lifted up on the cross, one of the two thieves was drawn to Him and saved. The centurion acknowledged Jesus as Son of God (Matt. 27:54). After Jesus was lifted up from the earth, that is, after resurrection, even now, people are drawn unto Him. Jesus also said, "And I, if I be lifted up from the earth, will draw all men unto me" (John 12:32). The devil's plan of destruction was turned into blessing.

Psalm 40:2 says:

> He brought me up also out of an horrible pit, out of the miry clay, and set my feet upon a rock, and established my goings.

Are you feeling low, like you are trapped in some horrible pit? Is your life going nowhere as though your feet were stuck in the clay? Then, turn to Jesus. He will lift you up.

Jesus Endured the Scourging for our Deliverance from Bondage

Then he said: "Cursed be Canaan; A servant of servants He shall be to his brethren."

—Genesis 9:25, NKJV

The Hebrew word for servant is *ebed*, which is also translated as "slave." It is used in the Bible for the first time in the above verse. Here Noah pronounces a curse on Canaan because of what his father Ham did to Noah.

Since that time men have tried to keep other men in slavery or bondage. One of the best examples of this is the Egyptians confining the Israelites to slavery.

Exodus 2:11 says:

And it came to pass in those days, when Moses was grown, that he went out unto his brethren, and looked on their burdens: and he spied an Egyptian smiting an Hebrew, one of his brethren.

Slaves must obey their masters. Disobedience can result in severe punishment. The Israelites were suffering under the whip of the cruel Egyptian taskmasters who were beating them down. As a result, they cried out to God. God broke the bondage of slavery.

Leviticus 26:13 (NKJV) describes:

I am the Lord your God who brought you out of the land of Egypt that you should not be their slaves, I have broken the band of your yoke and made you walk upright.

One day I happened to meet a young lady who was married to a very wealthy but very old man. When I discovered this fact during our conversation, I felt sorry for her because she was young and beautiful. When I asked her how she came to marry this man, her answer shocked me.

She told me that her father had taken a loan from this rich man and could not pay back the money. To settle the loan her father gave her in marriage to this rich man. In conservative families in India young girls generally obey their parents. This young girl simply obeyed her father and married this man who was old enough to be her grandfather. Now she is like a slave in the hands of this rich man.

Around the world, there are many people who cannot pay their debts and become slaves to their lenders. They must do what their masters say or else suffer the consequences.

Years ago in rural India, there prevailed the *Zamindari system*. The Zamindar would lend money at a very high rate of interest to poor farmers to buy seeds and other things needed to cultivate the lands. When the farmers failed to repay the loan, the Zamindar would take possession of their lands. These poor farmers and their families became laborers for the Zamindar. I thank God that such evil practices have now been eradicated in India.

In the Bible, there is a story about the prophet who could not pay his debt. When he died, the lender came to take away his children as slaves (2 Kings 4:1–7). But the widow cried out to the prophet Elisha to help her save her children. God did a great miracle by filling every vessel the widow could borrow with oil to sell and pay up the debt. In the modern world, literal slavery may not be very common, but the borrower is still a slave to the lender.

Today there are other types of slavery prevalent among

people. There are people who are addicted to drugs, alcohol, pornography, adultery, and so on. They become veritable slaves to these bad habits. But Jesus came into this world to liberate people from such slavery.

Because of the blood that Jesus shed from the wounds on His back, we are set free from the curse of slavery.

> Therefore you are no longer a slave but a son, and if a son, then an heir of God through Christ.
> —GALATIANS 4:7, NKJV

JESUS ENDURED THE SCOURGING IN ORDER TO FULFILL THE LAW

According to Deuteronomy 25:2, a wicked man deserved to be beaten. "And it shall be, if the wicked man be worthy to be beaten, that the judge shall cause him to lie down, and to be beaten before his face, according to his fault, by a certain number."

I believe that in this particular case the form of punishment was whipping by cane. The law stated that when a man disobeyed the law, according to the gravity of his fault he would be beaten a certain number of times. The maximum number of lashes was forty, but to avoid breaking the law themselves by miscount, they usually stopped at thirty-nine (Deut. 25:3).

But Jesus willingly endured more than what was required in the law in order to save us from the punishment which we deserve.

Years ago a missionary came to India and brought money with him for his ministry. But he needed to exchange the foreign currency into Indian currency so that he could feed

POWER AND PURPOSE IN THE WOUNDS OF JESUS

the lepers, clothe and educate the orphans, and preach the gospel to the poor.

He arranged a broker to conduct the transaction, but the police found it out and stopped it. You see, in India only government-authorized brokers can conduct foreign exchange transactions. What he was doing was against the law. The government officers detained the missionary and took him to the headquarters for questioning.

When the officers discovered the purpose of his visit and the noble cause, which he was supporting with the money, they did not prosecute him. Still the law had been broken and the law had to be fulfilled. And since ignorance of the law is no excuse, the missionary still had to be punished. It was decided that he would pay only a personal penalty so that the noble causes, which he supported, could continue.

In Matthew 5:17 Jesus says:

> Think not that I am come to destroy the law, or the prophets: I am not come to destroy, but to fulfill.

> To redeem them that were under the law, that we might receive the adoption as sons. And because ye are sons, God has sent forth the Spirit of his Son into your hearts, crying, Abba, Father.
> —GALATIANS 4:5–6

Because Jesus fulfilled the punishment required under law, we have been set free from all the punishments. The blood of Jesus that was shed from His back has set us free. Hallelujah!

Chapter 8
WOUNDS ON HIS CHEST

And one shall say to him, What are these wounds on your breast or between your hands? Then he will answer, Those with which I was wounded [when disciplined] in the house of my [loving] friends.
—ZECHARIAH 13:6, AMP

And if someone asks, "Then what are those scars on your chest?" he will say, "I was wounded at the home of friends!"
—ZECHARIAH 13:6, NLT

I N THE ABOVE verse, Prophet Zechariah refers to the wounds in between the hands. To make it clear, he speaks about the wounds in the chest.

The next verse (Zech. 13:7, NKJV) says, "Strike the shepherd, and the sheep will be scattered." Jesus foretold this to His disciples (Matt. 26:31–32), and it was fulfilled on the same night in the Garden of Gethsemane (Matt. 26:56).

Hence, I am of the view that Zechariah 13:6 speaks about the wounds in the chest of our Lord Jesus. Moreover, the following will make it very clear that our Lord was wounded in His chest.

As mentioned in earlier chapters, Psalm 22:12–18 speaks about the sufferings of Jesus and parallels what is described in the gospels. Verse 17 is especially interesting when it says, "I may count all my bones" (ASV).

Many years ago, while I was riding my motorcycle on a particular night, I did not notice a small ditch on the road. When my bike hit the ditch, I lost control and fell on the hand bar of my bike. I was in great pain, so I rushed to the hospital. Seeing my X-ray report, the doctors said that I had a mild fracture in one of my chest rib bones. From the X-ray, I could see the fracture and was also able to see and count all my bones.

How was it that Jesus could count His bones? To count them He must have been able to see them.

In an earlier chapter, I described the whip that was used to scourge Jesus. Embedded in the long heavy leather straps were pieces of metal and bone that protruded from the strap far enough to form sharp hooks. When the Roman soldier applied the whip to the back of Jesus, the leather straps wrapped around His body, striking the chest also.

Each time the whip was drawn back, the metal and bone hooks grabbed and tore pieces of skin and flesh from His chest. With the rib bones located just under the skin, it would not have been long before they were exposed. Then, the position of hanging on the cross would extend Jesus' view of His own chest, thus making the bones visible and exposing themselves to be counted.

Jesus was able to count His bones because His bosom was laid open by the blows, scourges, and wounds He received. Now why would the devil want to inflict this sort of injury to the bosom of Jesus?

Let us look at a few blessings we receive from His bosom based on Scripture.

He Carries Us on His
Bosom and Protects Us

Just because of His abundant love for the Israelites, God sent the angel of the Lord, who appeared to Moses in a flame of fire in the midst of a bush, so as to strengthen him to deliver thousands of people from the bondage of Pharaoh and to lead them on to the Promised Land. However, the Israelites forgot all the miracles the Lord did for them and murmured against Moses and the Lord. Moses was dejected. He cried to the Lord, "Did I conceive all these people? Did I beget them, that You should say to me, 'Carry them in your bosom, as a guardian carries a nursing child,' to the land which You swore to their fathers?" (Num. 11:12, NKJV). We find Moses saying that he had not conceived them to be carried on his bosom and then he confirms the fact that it is the Lord who had been carrying them in His bosom so far. So we come to know that God protects His children, keeping them in His bosom.

We know that a kangaroo protects its little one safely in its pouch and hops away in a hurry to protect it from enemies.

The bosom is considered a safe and secure place where your eyes can see and your hands protect. For example, in Eastern countries objects are carried in a fold in the garment near the bosom just as people in the West use pockets. In India, where I come from, men have a secret pocket inside their shirts to keep their valuables close to their hearts.

Isaiah 40:11 says, "He shall feed his flock like a shepherd: he shall gather the lambs with his arm, and carry them in his bosom, and shall gently lead those that are with young." This scripture speaks of Jesus as the Good Shepherd who carries His lambs in His bosom, tenderly caring for them and watching over them.

Isaiah 46:4 (NKJV) says, "I will carry you! I have made, and I will bear; Even I will carry, and will deliver you." From this scripture we know our God carries His beloved children in His bosom in order to protect them from their enemies.

HE COMFORTS HIS CHILDREN IN HIS BOSOM

When infants cry and fret, we see parents picking them up and pressing them to their bosoms. Instantly the infants stop crying, as they are greatly comforted.

In Luke 16:19–31 we read about a rich man and a beggar named Lazarus. Lazarus, full of sores, was laid at the gate of the rich man. He desired to be fed with the crumbs which fell from the rich man's table. Moreover, the dogs came and licked his sores. Both the beggar and the rich man died one day. The angels carried the beggar to the bosom of Abraham, but the rich man went down to Hades. He was tormented there and when he lifted his eyes, he saw the beggar in the bosom of Abraham. "He cried out, 'Father Abraham, have mercy on me, and send Lazarus that he may dip the tip of his finger in water and cool my tongue; for I am tormented in this flame.' But Abraham said, 'Son, remember that in your lifetime you received your good things, and likewise Lazarus evil things; but now he is comforted and you are tormented'" (Luke 16:24–25, NKJV). We learn from this parable that our Lord comforts those who suffer. Since He is the one who comforts us, His friend Abraham comforted Lazarus who had faced sufferings and sorrows.

We read this characteristic of our Lord being reflected in Isaiah 66:12–13: "Then you shall feed; on her sides shall you be carried and be dandled on her knees. As one whom his mother comforts, so I will comfort you; and you shall be comforted in Jerusalem" (NKJV).

Beloved! The Lord comforts everyone whom He loves, keeping them in His bosom.

HE REVEALS HIMSELF
KEEPING US IN HIS BOSOM

The spirit of the Lord was upon Samson in a very special mighty measure. When a young lion came roaring against him, he could tear the lion apart as one would have torn apart a young goat. Single-handedly he could kill thirty Philistines.

When the spirit of the Lord descended mightily upon him, the ropes that had bound his arms became like flax that burned with fire, and his bonds broke loose from his hands. He could kill 1,000 men with the fresh jawbone of a donkey. Samson, who was empowered by the special spirit of the Lord, opened his heart to Delilah who had befriended him and who was daily leaning on his bosom. Because of this, we see in the Bible how the mighty Samson lost all his strength (Judg. 16:17–18, 20).

If a woman who leans on the bosom of a human being can find out his secret, how much more can a believer who leans on His bosom learn from the Lord who loves him dearly?

We read in Isaiah 66:12 that the Lord feeds His children like a mother. Milk is the food for an infant. In the same way, the Lord keeps His children whom He loves to His bosom and feeds them with spiritual manna by revealing His secrets to them. Thus, He strengthens them. This is why pious and devoted believers stand zealous for our Lord. We know that our Lord Jesus loved His disciple John and he was leaning on the bosom of our Lord (John 13:23). I believe that is the reason why God revealed to John the events of the future on the island of Patmos. John eventually wrote the wonderful book of Revelation.

In my life, when my daughter went to be with the Lord in 2006, I made a choice to resort to the bosom of our Lord. He revealed a lot of hidden spiritual things in the Word of God. These spiritual revelations truly comforted me.

In short, as our Lord loves us, He keeps us in His bosom, to protect and comfort us and to reveal Himself to us.

Love Is Poured Out
from the Heart

I remember when my daughter Sharon was a baby, how I would carry her close to my bosom and walk slowly about the house until she fell asleep. She was safe and secure and felt loved in my arms.

Love is poured out from the heart (bosom). Lucifer was a cherubim and stayed close to God before he sinned. I believe that the devil purposely inflicted the wounds on His chest so that Jesus would not be able to keep His loved ones close to His bosom.

Naturally, when there is a wound on the chest it becomes painful and difficult to hug someone and hold him to your bosom. But the blood, which He shed from the wounds in His chest, has the power to draw you into His bosom.

By sending His Son to be the propitiation for our sins, God revealed His love for us (1 John 4:9–10). The Bible tells us that God is love and that His love is revealed through His Son Jesus Christ (John 3:16).

Each and every one of the wounds on His body, particularly the wounds on His bosom, was the outcome of His love for us. Our Lord revealed His love for us on the cross. After He was tormented, crucified, and buried, He came as the resurrected Savior to Peter and asked him thrice, "Do you love me?" Do we love the Lord who revealed His love for us through His wounds? Have we revealed and reflected our love towards Him?

In a marriage relationship, both the husband and wife must express their love for one another and receive love from each other. Otherwise, their love is not complete. In the same way, if we do not express our love for Him, our love is not complete.

We may say that we love God, but how do we express that love for Him?

We express our love for God by believing in His Son Jesus.

> For the Father Himself loves you, because you have loved Me, and have believed that I came forth from God.
>
> —JOHN 16:27, NKJV

We express our love for God by obeying His Word.

> Jesus answered and said to him, "If anyone loves Me, he will keep My word; and My Father will love him, and We will come to him and make Our home with him."
>
> —JOHN 14:23, NKJV

We express our love for God by receiving the Holy Spirit. God also expresses His love for us by giving us the Holy Spirit.

Now hope does not disappoint, because the love of
God has been poured out in our hearts by the Holy
Spirit who was given to us.
—ROMANS 5:5, NKJV

When we reveal our love to Him, Jesus will keep us in His
bosom where He will carry and protect us, comfort us and
keep us in a close personal relationship, and reveal Himself to
us. The blood from His bosom will bring all these blessings.

Chapter 9
PLUCKED OFF HIS HAIR

*He was oppressed, and he was afflicted, yet he opened not his
mouth: he is brought as a lamb to the slaughter, and as a sheep
before her shearers is dumb, so he openeth not his mouth.*

—ISAIAH 53:7

THERE ARE SOME who believe that when Pilate
ordered Jesus to be scourged, he considered it to be
Jesus' final punishment. It was only after the taunts
by the Jewish mob questioning Pilate's loyalty to Caesar that
Pilate delivered Jesus to be crucified (John 19:12). Therefore,
the scourging should have been thorough.

Jesus was stripped of His clothing and severely beaten.
When the scourging was over, the soldiers mocked Jesus.
They placed a crown of thorns on His head and threw a robe
across His shoulders before returning Him to Pilate. Jesus
was still wearing the robe when Pilate presented Him to the
Jews (John 19:2–5).

While this was going on, the blood from Jesus' wounds
would have soaked the robe and would have begun to clot,
causing the robe to stick to His body. After Pilate delivered
Jesus to be crucified, the soldiers took off the robe from His
body (Mark 15:20). Not only would this have caused excruciating pain, but it would have also plucked pieces of skin,

flesh, and even hair from His body like when a bandage is carelessly ripped from a wound.

Also, in his attempt to scourge Jesus thoroughly, the Roman soldier would have applied the whip to the entire body of Jesus. It is possible that the whip could have struck Jesus on the face, plucking the hairs from His cheeks. The act of placing the crown of thorns on His head and the numerous blows of the rod by the Roman soldiers could have caused Jesus' hairs to be yanked out.

Upon seeing Jesus coming towards him, John the Baptist declared:

> Behold! The Lamb of God that takes away the sins of the world!
>
> —JOHN 1:29, NKJV

Isaiah 53:7 says:

> He was oppressed, and he was afflicted, yet he opened not his mouth: he is brought as a lamb to the slaughter, and as a sheep before her shearers is dumb, so he openeth not his mouth.

These passages of Scripture paint a word picture of our Lord as a lamb being led to the slaughter. Isaiah clearly states that the lamb will be shorn before it is slaughtered. He had prophesied that every hair from His body would be uprooted before He was crucified.

Isaiah 50:6 says, "I gave my back to the smiters, and my cheeks to them that plucked off the hair; I hid not my face from shame and spitting." We can see that even the hair on His cheeks was plucked off.

Jesus Christ, the Lamb of God, willingly allowed Himself

to be stripped of all He had just like the lamb that is about to be slaughtered and a sheep before its shearers is dumb. He was like a shorn sheep under the hands of its shearer, to be slaughtered and sacrificed for the sins of His people, so as to fulfill the Scriptures.

During His ordeal, even the very hair on Jesus' body was plucked out. Why was the devil so eager to abuse Jesus even down to this smallest of details? Let us meditate on this as we look at the Scriptures.

Hair Is a Symbol of the Anointing and Power of God

The life of Samson is presented to us in the book of Judges from chapters 13 through 16.

Even before Samson was born, an angel of the Lord appeared to his mother and told her that "…no razor shall come on his head: for the child shall be a Nazarite unto God from the womb: and he shall begin to deliver Israel out of the hand of the Philistines" (Judg. 13:5).

Thus from his birth no razor came on the head of Samson. When he accosted a lion, the Bible says, "He rent him as he would have rent a kid, and he had nothing in his hand" (Judg. 14:6).

On yet another occasion, "He found a new jawbone of an ass, and put forth his hand, and took it, and slew a thousand men therewith" (Judg. 15:15).

Thus, Samson fought against the Philistines, who were the enemies of Israel, with supernatural strength.

When Delilah pressed him daily to disclose the source of his strength until his "soul was vexed unto death" (Judg. 16:16), Samson finally blurted out his secret that his strength lay in his locks. Delilah promptly got Samson's seven locks shaved and Samson was a spent force thereafter. Samson's supernatural strength was in the hair of his head.

While our Lord Jesus sojourned on this earth, He also demonstrated supernatural power. He walked on water, rebuked the wind and the sea, causing the stormy ocean to become quiet. Jesus transformed water into tasty wine and fed five thousand men with just five loaves of bread and two fish. He healed lepers, gave sight to the blind, and opened the ears of the deaf. He made the lame people walk, dumb speak, and raised some who were dead.

Perhaps the devil was bewildered and could not understand the source of Jesus' supernatural strength. He might have guessed that like Samson, all of Jesus' strength was in the hair on His head. Thus, he planned to pluck Jesus' hair, thinking that he could cut the source of His power.

The devil knows that he cannot establish his kingdom on this earth because of Jesus. Could this be the reason why the devil caused the Roman soldiers to scourge Jesus so severely? Did he intend to strip the anointing on Jesus by plucking His hair?

THE PLUCKING OF JESUS' HAIR SYMBOLICALLY BROKE THE GRIP OF SATAN

In the book of Revelation, the disciple John describes the locusts that came from the bottomless pit. These locusts were given power like that of scorpions of the earth. They wore something like crowns of gold, and their faces resembled human faces. Their hair was like women's hair, and their teeth were like a lion's teeth. They had breastplates like the breastplates of iron, and the sound of their wings was like the thundering of many horses and chariots rushing into battle. They had tails and stings like scorpions, and in their tails they had power to torment people. They had a king over them, which is the angel of the bottomless pit (Rev. 9:3–11). In this portion, we can see that the destroying locusts' hair was like the hair of women.

There is beauty in a woman's long hair (1 Cor. 11:15). What God created for good, the devil always uses for a different purpose. The devil uses the hair of women to attract and bind the people.

Once a servant of God went to a particular place to do God's work. It was a very hard "ground." People were very violent and riotous; looting and other hideous crimes were very common in that place. This man of God cried to God to bring a revival in that area. In a vision, he saw that the hair of the woman in the bottomless pit had tied many people in that place. This man of God understood that he needed God's power to cut the hair of Satan to release these people. When he sincerely prayed, God gave him an anointing to do God's work in that place. Our Lord used this man of God mightily to bring deliverance, healing, comfort, peace, and blessings in that place.

I have heard testimonies of people who used to practice witchcraft, but are now serving God saying that they used the hairs of people for witchcraft. It is common in India to see the hairs of devil-possessed people tied to certain trees. Though I do not find any Scripture to explain how these people use the hairs to bind others, I am certain that Satan does bind people, and that is why people are not able to come out of their addiction to alcohol, drugs, pornography, adultery, gambling, and so on. Satan has put his yoke around their necks. Wherever Satan pulls, people just follow him, and whatever Satan dictates, they simply obey him.

We saw that the supernatural power (the anointing) of

Samson was in his hair and that is why, in the same manner, Satan wanted to pluck every hair from our Lord Jesus. Symbolically we can say that hair represents anointing.

Isaiah 10:27 says: "And it shall come to pass in that day, that his burden shall be taken away from off thy shoulder, and his yoke from off thy neck, and the yoke shall be destroyed because of the anointing." God allowed Jesus' hair (anointing) to be plucked off, so that through His anointing God can break every yoke on the neck of people. We can say that Jesus gave His hair so that He could deliver the people who are bound by Satan. Here again, Jesus has brought blessings into our life.

PLUCKING OFF THE HAIR SIGNALS EXCOMMUNICATION FROM SOCIETY

In Nehemiah 13:25, we read, "And I contended with them, and cursed them, and smote certain of them, and plucked off their hair, and made them swear by God, saying, Ye shall not give your daughters unto their sons, nor take their daughters unto your sons, or for yourselves."

In some Indian villages, when a criminal is convicted of a crime, the village leaders would order his head to be shaved and would parade him around the village, bringing disgrace to him and his entire family.

In real life and in literature, there are several instances of wrongdoers being excommunicated from society. Even in the Bible, we read that those who were afflicted with leprosy were excommunicated. We know that our Lord Jesus was crucified along with two criminals outside the gates of the city of Jerusalem (Heb. 13:12).

Our Lord Jesus gave His sacred blood and even His hairs

in order to give life to those who face such situations in society.

The plucking off of hair was one of the signs indicating excommunication and separation from the congregation. Did the devil intend to separate Jesus from the church He has established on this earth in this manner? In Matthew 10:30, Jesus says, "But the very hairs of your head are all numbered" (NKJV). Moreover, in Luke 21:18 we read, "But not a hair of your head shall be lost" (NKJV).

When we start losing hair, it is natural for us to worry over this loss. However, for most of us, the hair falls from our heads even without our knowledge. It is true that we cannot count the number of hairs on our heads. But the Scripture says that our Lord has numbered our hairs, and not even one hair will fall without His permission or knowledge. If He is concerned about even our hair, just imagine the depth of His love for us!

Jesus allowed Himself to be shorn of His hair for our sake so that we may inherit His blessings. So let us be faithful and be thankful to Him. May our Lord God bless us! Amen!

Chapter 10
STRIPPED OF HIS CLOTHES

And they crucified him, and parted his garments, casting lots: that it might be fulfilled which was spoken by the prophet, They parted my garments among them, and upon my vesture did they cast lots.
—MATTHEW 27:35

S PROPHESIED BY King David in Psalm 22:18, the Roman soldiers took the garments of Jesus Christ and parted them among themselves. Let us examine the Scriptures to see the symbolic meaning behind this incident.

The people called Jesus Christ the son of David, Messiah, King of the Jews, Rabbi, and Son of God. Many people adored and followed Him. He was highly respected by His disciples. Nevertheless, the Roman soldiers stripped Him. "They stripped him and put a scarlet robe on him" (Matt. 27:28, NIV). The literal meaning of "strip" is to deprive, to plunder, to deprive of covering, to strip a man of his position, his rights, and his privileges. It is such a disgrace to a person when other people strip him of his garments.

In the previous chapter, we also saw that when the Roman soldiers stripped Jesus of His blood-soaked garment, Jesus' hair was also plucked along with the garments from His body, and this would have caused searing pain to our Lord Jesus.

If we read the Scriptures diligently, we can notice that the garment of our Lord was taken away from Him three times.

- First, before He was flogged (Matt. 27:28)
- Second, after Jesus was mocked (Matt. 27:31)
- Third, before He was crucified (Matt. 27:35)

What was the intention of the devil in directing the Roman soldiers to strip Jesus three times in a row? Let us study how our Lord transformed this evil design of the devil into a blessing.

According to the plan shown by God (Exod. 25:18–20), Moses made two cherubim of gold on the top of the ark of covenant with the cherubim spreading out their wings overshadowing the mercy seat and facing one another. It was glorious for the cherubim to stand in the presence of the Lord in the most holy place. As the guardian cherubim were made of gold, we know that God had adorned them with special glory. They stood with their wings covering the mercy seat to symbolize the act of protection. It is not that they were protecting God, because God never needs protection. I believe that they were kept there to protect the people, lest they be destroyed by the presence of God.

When we analyze the following scriptures, we can see that there was another guardian cherub in the presence of God, who turned to be a traitor.

> "Son of man, take up a lamentation for the king of Tyre, and say to him, 'Thus says the Lord God: "You were the seal of perfection, full of wisdom and perfect in beauty. You were in Eden, the garden of God; every precious stone was your covering: The sardius, topaz, and diamond, beryl, onyx, and jasper, sapphire,

turquoise, and emerald with gold. The workmanship of your timbrels and pipes was prepared for you on the day you were created. You were the anointed cherub who covers; I established you; you were on the holy mountain of God; you walked back and forth in the midst of fiery stones. You were perfect in your ways from the day you were created, till iniquity was found in you. By the abundance of your trading you became filled with violence within, and you sinned; therefore I cast you as a profane thing out of the mountain of God; and I destroyed you, O covering cherub, from the midst of the fiery stones. Your heart was lifted up because of your beauty; you corrupted your wisdom for the sake of your splendor; I cast you to the ground, I laid you before kings that they might gaze at you. You defiled your sanctuaries by the multitude of your iniquities, By the iniquity of your trading; therefore I brought fire from your midst; it devoured you, and I turned you to ashes upon the earth in the sight of all who saw you.'"

—Ezekiel 28:12–18, NKJV

Although the above verses appear to prophesy the fate of the king of Tyre, how can he become the anointed guardian cherub? How could Tyre's king be in the Garden of Eden? How could he walk in the midst of the stones of fire, in the presence of God? When we ponder over these things, we understand that this passage refers to Lucifer. The Bible scholars too infer that it is Lucifer who is being referred to here.

Lucifer was a guardian cherub clothed in the glory of God in the presence of God. The day he sinned, he was cast from the mountain of God, and he lost his glory. With this in mind, let us now examine the reason why Satan instigated the soldiers to strip the clothes of our Lord.

GARMENT OF PROTECTION

People wear clothes to suit the weather. In India people wear cotton clothes during summer and woolen clothes or clothes made of leather during winter. Soldiers' protective outfits are meant to protect them during wartime while athletes dress in such a way so that they will not be injured during a game.

When I thought about the fact that clothes provide protection for man, I was reminded of this incident which I would like to share with you. In Pasumalai, a town in Tamil Nadu, India, where I was brought up, every year during the Holy week, the community would re-enact the life of Jesus through a play called "Love Divine." During the scene in which Jesus is beaten, the actor who plays the role of Jesus would wear clothes that were slightly padded to protect himself from the "thrashing" by the soldiers.

Our God, who dwells in the midst of inseparable light, created all things. He created Lucifer as the crown of perfection, full of wisdom and beauty. Lucifer walked on the holy mountain of God in the midst of the stones of fire. He was placed in the presence of God as an anointed guardian cherub (Ezek. 28:12–17).

A soldier who is posted in the border of a country receives authority from the government to protect his country. He is clothed in a uniform showing his rank. That attire gives him authority to shoot and kill enemies that try to cross the border; he is not sentenced to death for killing the enemies, instead the government honors him. At the same time, if the soldier who has to safeguard his country becomes a traitor, the government withdraws not only his authority, but also the privileges given to him. He would be punished for his crime. Likewise, when the anointed guardian cherub committed the sin of profaning the sanctuary of God, God removed the anointing, the protection, and the garment of glory from him, and He brought forth fire from the midst of him and said he would be consumed to ashes (Ezek. 28:18).

The guardian cherub became a thief, and the Bible tells us that the thief comes only to steal, kill, and destroy and not for anything else (John 10:10).

As long as sin was not found in him, Lucifer was dressed gorgeously (Ezek. 28:13). But when Lucifer was cast away, he was stripped of his garments, that is, the anointing which was in him, or the presence of God, the fire and the light, were all taken away from him. In short, divine protection was removed from him, and he was cast into darkness.

Satan knew that healing power came from the garment of Jesus (Mark 5:27–29). He might have thought that the supernatural power of protection was also in the garment of Jesus. By stripping Jesus of His clothes, Satan could have imagined that he had taken away the divine protection Jesus had from God.

The Bible tells us that no one can approach or get near our Holy God (1 Tim. 6:16). First Samuel 6:20 says, "Who is able to stand before this holy LORD God?" (NKJV). However, by the mercy of God, Jesus has made a way for us to enter into God's presence. It is not our righteousness that makes us worthy to stand in His presence (Isa. 64:6), but His blood that has made us righteous before Him (Rom. 5:9).

In the parable of the marriage of the king's son (Matt. 22:1–14), the guests who were called were required to wear the wedding garment. When the king found a person who did not wear this garment, he ordered his servants to bind that guest and cast him into outer darkness. From this parable, we infer that one requires a special garment to participate in the wedding of the Lamb, that is, to stand in His presence. I believe that only the person who wears this garment dipped in the blood (Rev. 19:13), that is, the garment of salvation and the robe of His righteousness (Isa. 61:10) is worthy to stand in the presence of God. This garment of Jesus protects a person from perishing because of the holiness of God.

When we analyze the symbolic meaning of why the Roman soldiers shared the garment of Jesus, we can see that Jesus gave His garment so that we could wear it and stand before the Holy God. Jesus' clothes were stripped so that we could be clothed with divine protection. His garment on the one hand protects us from perishing in His presence, and on the other hand, it protects us from evil (Luke 10:19) and from sickness (Exod. 15:26; Ps. 91:3, 10; Matt. 8:17).

GARMENT OF GLORY

Most people are able to infer the standard of living of a man by merely looking at the brand of clothes he wears, and they respect him accordingly. "And you shall make holy garments for Aaron your brother for glory and for beauty" (Exod. 28:2, NKJV).

When King Nebuchadnezzar became arrogant and his heart hardened with pride, he was deposed from the royal throne and stripped of his glory by God (Dan. 5:20). In the same way when Satan sinned, his glory was taken away from him. Ezekiel 28:13 says that Satan was dressed in gorgeous clothes, but he lost his clothes of glory because of his sin.

In the beginning, God created Adam and Eve in His own image, and placed them in the Garden of Eden. He had crowned them with His glory. "Yet thou hast made him a little less than God, and dost crown him with glory and honour" (Ps. 8:5). But the day they sinned, they lost the glory of God (Rom. 3:23). At that time, their earthly eyes opened. They realized that they were naked and were not worthy to stand before God.

Even today, Satan tries to strip us of our divine clothes, and thus make us unworthy to stand before our Lord. But God covers our nakedness, and we become His (Ezek. 16:8).

Furthermore, we read in Revelation 3:18 how God asks us to get clothed in white garments to cover our nakedness. As Satan was stripped of his glory, he wanted to strip Jesus of His clothes and pass on his disgrace to our Lord Jesus.

In the Garden of Eden, all the needs of Adam and Eve were met. However, when they sinned, God drove them away. Therefore, to meet their needs, they had to work hard until their sweat fell to the ground. Poverty came to humanity because of sin. But God took upon Himself the poverty which befell man as a result of sin. Jesus took this poverty upon Himself when He was stripped of His clothes. As a result, He has made us rich: "For you know the grace of our Lord Jesus Christ that though He was rich, yet for your sakes He became poor, that you through His poverty might become rich" (2 Cor. 8:9, NKJV).

Though I was born and brought up in a Christian family, I was not taught the importance of giving. I learned the importance of giving only when I accepted our Lord as my personal Savior. In 1988, I received an award from the government of India, a sum of 50,000 rupees (nearly $1,000) and I decided to give my church an offering of 5000 rupees ($100) for the building fund. In those days it was a very big sum for me, and that was the biggest offering I had given until then. I decided to obey God's Word. After I gave the offering, when I came out of the church and started my bike, suddenly felt as if our Lord was putting a robe on me. I truly rejoiced at the strange feeling and the presence of God. From then on, I could see the Lord's blessing flowing into my life. Today our Lord has not only made me a debt-free man, but He has also made me a blessing to many people. Our Lord took away poverty and made me rich both in my spiritual and material lives.

Many crimes are committed against women. There are cases when they are molested and overpowered by their attackers. The victim is helpless and feels bereft of any self-respect. Jesus can understand the victim's feeling. His garments, too, were stripped by His enemy. He gave his garment so as to remove such disgrace and clothe the victim with His glory.

Christ having lost His clothes before His crucifixion has given us the garment of glory originally lost by Adam and Eve, and thus has made us not only worthy to stand before God, but has also made us kings and priests before God (Rev. 1:6). His sufferings are meant to be blessings to us.

GARMENT OF PRAISE

On carefully studying the scriptures which speak about Lucifer (Ezek. 28:12–17; Isa. 14:12–14), we find that he was adorned by musical instruments such as pipes (wind instruments) and precious stones on the day he was created:

> Thou hast been in Eden the garden of God; every precious stone was thy covering, the sardius, topaz, and the diamond, the beryl, the onyx, and the jasper, the sapphire, the emerald, and the carbuncle, and gold: the workmanship of thy tabrets and of thy pipes was prepared in thee in the day that thou wast created.
>
> —EZEKIEL 28:13

91

We know that God created all things with a purpose. In the Bible, we see people used instruments to sing songs of praise to God. I believe that God had clothed Lucifer with the garment of praise so that he could be the worshiper in God's presence.

Many theologians have also opined that Lucifer was the worship leader, and when he sinned he was pushed down from his position. Isaiah 14:15 says, "But you are brought down to the grave, to the depths of the pit" (NIV). Moreover, Matthew 8:12 portrays this as a place of darkness, and there will be weeping and gnashing of teeth. Satan was thrown down to this pit.

When I went to Israel, I had the privilege of going to the church of St. Peter in Gallicantu, where Peter is said to have denied Jesus thrice. It was the courtyard of Caiaphas then. It is believed that Jesus spent the last night of His earthly life in a small concave place below the ground level (that is, a pit) in this place. A Bible has been placed there on a pulpit and is opened to Psalm 102. It is a psalm of an afflicted man and when overwhelmed, he pours out his complaint before the Lord. When I stood there and read this psalm, it helped me understand a little of the grief and loneliness Jesus would have gone through that night.

"When I put on sackcloth, people make sport of me" (Ps. 69:11, NIV). In the Bible, we see that when the people of that time mourned, they tore their clothes, put on sackcloth, and put ashes on their heads. In mourning, our Lord, too, put on the sackcloth. In other words, the Lord who is worthy of praise, was made to enter the pit to experience grief, mourning, and loneliness. Satan would have rejoiced at this.

Jesus had to go through this valley of mourning to clothe

us with the garment of praise. Isaiah 61:3 (emphasis added) says:

> To appoint unto them that mourn in Zion, to give unto them beauty for ashes, the oil of joy for mourning, *the garment of praise* for the spirit of heaviness; that they might be called trees of righteousness, the planting of the LORD, that he might be glorified.

There is a dear family in Malaysia who takes care of me as their own son. In the year 1998, all of a sudden the head of the family went to be with the Lord. As his wife cried bitterly, she heard a voice saying, "What prevents you from worshiping me?" Immediately she knelt down, raised her hands and began to praise God. Her grief left her instantaneously.

There are many such moments of grief and pain we go through in our lives. However, our Lord bore all our grief and thus clothed us with the garment of praise. No matter what circumstances you face in your life, put on the garment of praise and you will surely get a breakthrough. The Bible describes that God inhabits the praises of His children (Ps. 22:3).

God allowed Jesus' garments to be stripped by His enemies so that He can clothe us with the garment of protection (salvation), the garment of glory (a kingly and priestly garment), and the garment of praise, so that we can be in His presence forever.

Chapter 11
WOUNDS IN JESUS' HEART

My heart is wounded within me.

—PSALM 109:22

*Many bulls surround me; strong bulls of Bashan encircle me. Roaring lions
tearing their prey open their mouths wide against me. I am poured out
like water, and all my bones are out of joint. My heart has turned to wax;
it has melted away within me. My strength is dried up like a potsherd, and
my tongue sticks to the roof of my mouth; you lay me in the dust of death.*

—PSALM 22:12–15, NIV

IN THE ABOVE passage, we can see that King David, filled
with the Spirit of God, prophesied about the sufferings
of our Lord Jesus Christ. He says that many strong
bulls of Bashan will encircle our Lord and roaring lions will
open their mouths wide in order to tear their prey. Though
this portion portrays the physical sufferings of our Lord, we
may infer that the lions opening their mouths signify the
verbal abuse that our Lord had to bear when He came into
this world.

Here is the scripture that shows the fulfilment of this
⸢prop⸣hecy: "Then the soldiers of the governor took Jesus into
⸢the prae⸣torium and gathered the whole garrison around

Him. And they stripped Him and put a scarlet robe on Him. When they had twisted a crown of thorns, they put it on His head, and a reed in His right hand. And they bowed the knee before Him and mocked Him, saying, 'Hail, King of the Jews!' Then they spat on Him, and took the reed and struck Him on the head. And when they had mocked Him, they took the robe off Him, put His own clothes on Him, and led Him away to be crucified" (Matt. 27:27–31, NKJV).

The same incident has also been recorded by Mark in his gospel (Mark 15:15–20). The entire brigade in Pilate's palace gathered around Jesus. They stripped Him of His clothes and put on Him a scarlet robe, wove thorn-branches into a crown and pressed it on His head, and placed a scepter in His right hand and mocked Him saying, "Hail, King of the Jews."

We read in Luke 22 that those soldiers not only mocked our Lord Jesus, but also insulted Him using evil and slanderous words. "Now the men who had Jesus in custody treated Him with contempt and scoffed at and ridiculed Him and beat Him; they blindfolded Him also and asked Him, Prophesy! Who is it that struck You? And they said many other evil and slanderous and insulting words against Him, reviling Him" (Luke 22:63-65, AMP). King Herod also joined with his soldiers in ridiculing Jesus and mocking Him. "And Herod, with his soldiers, treated Him with contempt and scoffed at and ridiculed Him; then, dressing Him up in bright and gorgeous apparel, he sent Him back to Pilate" (Luke 23:11, AMP).

When our Lord Jesus was wounded, beaten up, and hung on the cross, the Roman rulers sneered at Him. Even the people who stood by watching sneered at Him. Luke 23:35 says, "Now the people stood by [calmly and leisurely] watching; but the rulers scoffed and sneered (turned up their noses) at Him, saying, 'He rescued others [from death]; let Him now rescue Himself, if He is the Christ (the Messiah) of God, His Chosen One!'" (AMP).

As we ponder over the above verses from the Scriptures we are able to realize that our Lord Jesus not only suffered physical torture, but was also ridiculed, mocked, insulted and cursed. Those words of mockery and curses made the heart of our Lord melt like wax (Ps. 22:14). The reproach of the people broke the heart of our Lord: "Reproach has broken my heart, and I am full of heaviness; I looked for someone to take pity, but there was none; And for comforters, but I found none" (Ps. 69:20, NKJV). The wounds of His heart weakened Him and He became like a potsherd (Ps. 22:15).

Let us now look into the reasons why Satan instigated the people to verbally abuse or curse Jesus.

In the Garden of Eden, after our first father and mother ate the fruit of the forbidden tree, our Lord God asked Adam, "Did you eat the forbidden fruit?" In the same way God asked Eve, "Why did you do this?" But the Lord did not ask Satan, the serpent, any question, but cursed him (Gen. 3:11–14). The Lord asked Adam and Eve the reason for their disobedience. But He did not ask Satan the reason for deceiving Adam and Eve, but He cursed Satan immediately. When the Lord cursed him, Satan not only lost his form, but he was also humiliated with a change of food—being bidden to eat dust.

> And He said, "Who told you that you were naked? Have you eaten from the tree of which I commanded you that you should not eat?" Then the man said, "The woman whom You gave to be with me, she gave me of the tree, and I ate." And the LORD God said to the woman, "What is this you have done?" The woman said, "The serpent deceived me, and I ate." So the

LORD God said to the serpent: "Because you have done
this, you are cursed more than all cattle, and more than
every beast of the field; On your belly you shall go, and
you shall eat dust all the days of your life."

—GENESIS 3:11–14, NKJV

The Almighty God is the one who created the angels (even
the fallen angels) and human beings. The Lord has fashioned
a path for the salvation of human beings, whereas He did not
make a way for the salvation of Satan. (I have discussed the
reasons in Chapter 1 "Wounds by the Crown of Thorns.")

Now let us ponder over the following verses and analyze
why Satan verbally abused Jesus. Such verses reveal that our
Lord had rebuked or cursed Satan.

In Genesis 3:14 (NKJV) mentioned above, we read:

So the LORD God said to the serpent: "Because you have
done this, you *are* cursed more than all cattle, and more
than every beast of the field; on your belly you shall go,
and you shall eat dust all the days of your life."

In Zechariah 3:1–2 (NKJV) we read:

Then he showed me Joshua the high priest standing
before the Angel of the LORD, and Satan standing at
his right hand to oppose him. And the LORD said to
Satan, "The LORD rebuke you, Satan! The LORD who
has chosen Jerusalem rebuke you! Is this not a brand
plucked from the fire?"

Jude 1:9 (NKJV) reads:

Yet Michael the archangel, in contending with the devil,
when he disputed about the body of Moses, dared not

bring against him a reviling accusation, but said, "The Lord rebuke you!"

Satan is said to be the ruler of this world (John 14:30). If so, would he not have felt dishonored when he was scolded and cursed? As Satan was rebuked by God, he showed his anger against Jesus by instigating men to ridicule Him. He made men hurt our Lord with words. Words are powerful and can build or destroy a man (Prov. 18:21). When people taunt us, our spirits wither away.

An example of this state of man can be seen in Psalm 102: "My enemies reproach me all day long; those who deride me swear an oath against me. For I have eaten ashes like bread, and mingled my drink with weeping, because of Your indignation and Your wrath; For You have lifted me up and cast me away. My days are like a shadow that lengthens, and I wither away like grass" (Ps. 102:8–11, NKJV).

In the book of Nehemiah, we read "But it so happened, when Sanballat heard that we were rebuilding the wall, that he was furious and very indignant, and mocked the Jews. And he spoke before his brethren and the army of Samaria, and said, 'What are these feeble Jews doing? Will they fortify themselves? Will they offer sacrifices? Will they complete it in a day? Will they revive the stones from the heaps of rubbish–stones that are burned?' Now Tobiah the Ammonite was beside him, and he said, 'Whatever they build, if even a fox goes upon it, he will break down their stone wall'" (Neh. 4:1–3). These words of insult and mockery brought weariness to the Israelites who were working enthusiastically to rebuild the walls.

Sennacherib, King of Assyria, sent a huge army under three commanders against Jerusalem despite King Hezekiah's paying his taxes. The Rabshakeh, one of the commanders, ridiculed the confidence that King Hezekiah had in the Lord. Though the palace administrator, the secretary, and the recorder in the king's palace requested the commander of the Assyrian army to speak in Aramaic and not in Hebrew, the Rabshakeh defied them and spoke purposely in Hebrew, the language of Judah, so that the people of that nation could hear those words of humiliation. He spoke in Hebrew to dishearten the people by instructing them not to put their trust in King Hezekiah or their God Jehovah (2 Kings 18:26–27). Here, the words were used as "a sword" to break the spirit of the people of Jerusalem.

I would like to narrate an incident from my life, which took place in the field of sports. This will show how harsh words can wreak havoc in a person's mind. Having represented the university and State field hockey teams, I got a job as an officer in the Customs and Excise Department in India and started playing for my office field hockey team. One day, we played against a team which had five players who were representatives of the Indian Olympics hockey team. Of course, they were a far better team than we were. In a few minutes after the start of the game, we scored a goal. The opponents started playing with great vigor and speed and attacked us, but they could not score the equalizer. While the match was in progress, I, as the goalkeeper of our team, committed a foul against my opponents. Though my action did not greatly affect the game, my captain reprimanded me in the presence of everyone. Those words broke my spirit and I could not play as well as I had done before. This paved the way for the opponents to score the equalizer, and the match which we ought to have won ended in a draw.

Today, we see Satan working behind the scenes instigating

people to rebuke us with their piercing words. Those fiery words from people can break our spirits. Many of us end up not being able to run the race that the Lord has ordained for us, and we continue to face failures in our lives.

I, too, have had my share of trials and struggles. In 2006, I was threatened by gangsters. This experience greatly affected my family and fear gripped us. We could see the fear in the faces of our children who dreaded the fact that their father was facing danger. In the midst of this, both my children had to write their examinations—one for a tenth grade exam and the other for a junior college final. Halfway through his examinations, my son was affected by shingles in his right eye. He could not study for his examinations and had to sit alone in a separate room in the school to write his exam. At the same time, my wife who was working in a government department, was all of a sudden transferred to another city some 90 miles from our house, and it took nearly three hours to reach her new place of work. Soon after this, my father passed away. And then my wife fell down and ruptured her Achilles tendon. On top of this, she had to undergo a major surgery and was bedridden for more than four months.

In the midst of these challenges, we came face-to-face with a heart-breaking incident. My beloved daughter, who was just 16 years of age, suddenly died. Many people became very judgmental, and they wounded us with their piercing words. Some started ridiculing us mercilessly even as we were going through the valley of tears and experiencing excruciating pain in our lives for months on end. In all these trials, it was the immense grace of our precious Lord that upheld us. It is His strength that is enabling us to continue in His ministry to this day.

In the beginning of 2008, one day after conducting some

ministry, I returned to the place where I was staying. That night, the devil stood before me and started to rebuke me with foul words. As he was cursing me, I was wondering why the devil would want to curse me after I had undergone so much pain and suffering. My spirit began to wilt then. It was at that same moment that I could feel the Spirit of the Lord strengthening me, and I was not at all dismayed because of the tongue-lashing of the devil. Since our Lord Jesus Himself has gone through this path of suffering, He understands the pain in our hearts, and He is the only One who can sustain us.

I would like to elaborate on another aspect of this subject. There are many ways in which a man's heart is wounded. However, one of the things that can hurt a person most is when he feels remorse for his past mistakes which might have played havoc in his or others' lives.

Let me share with you an incident from the life of King David as an example. King David had instructed his army commander Joab to take a census of the fighting men in Israel and Judah. Though Joab had advised him against taking such a census, King David still overruled Joab. Following the census, Joab gave King David his report on the number of fighting men in Israel. God was displeased with the census and so punished Israel for it. The Lord sent a plague among the people, and seventy thousand people in the nation died. When David saw the people being punished so badly, all because of his sin, his conscience disturbed him greatly. So David prayed to the Lord saying, "I am the one who has sinned and done wrong. These my sheep what have they done? Let Your hand fall upon me and my family" (2 Sam. 24:17, NIV).

Like David, the mistakes we have committed or the wrong

decisions we have made in the past and which have affected others, can end up hurting us.

The Scripture says that our Lord Jesus Himself suffered like us (Heb. 2:18 and 4:15). When I was meditating on how Jesus' heart would have been wounded, the Holy Spirit showed me certain incidents in Jesus' life.

The incidents related to the pain He felt are: when the temple of God was made into a marketplace (Matt. 21:13); when the people were trying to find fault with His words (Matt. 22:15–18); when His own family members rejected Him (John 7:3–5); when Judas, one of His own disciples, betrayed Him for thirty pieces of silver coin (Matt. 26:15; Luke 22:47–48); when all the disciples left Him alone in the garden of Gethsemane (Mark 14:50); when the people who had received good things from the Lord asked Herod to release the murderer Barrabas; when His own people sought to kill Him (Matt. 16:16–23); and so on. While we can go on analyzing the various incidents that would have broken Jesus' heart, I would like to share with you one particular incident that would have greatly wounded Him.

In Matthew 2:1–18, we see that the wise men from the east came to Jerusalem to worship the infant Jesus. On hearing their views of Jesus' birth, King Herod was troubled that the King of Jews was born in his territory. He sent these wise men to Bethlehem to find the child and to bring word back to him so that he too could go and "worship" Him. When the wise men left the king's palace, they saw the same star, and it guided them to the place where Jesus was. The wise men bowed before the child and worshiped Him. After that, having been warned in a dream not to go back to Herod, they returned to their country by another route.

After they left, being warned by the angel of the Lord,

Joseph took the child Jesus and Mary to Egypt. When Herod heard that he had been outwitted by the wise men, he was furious and he gave orders to kill all the male children in Bethlehem and in the vicinity who were two years old and under (Matt. 2:16).

Would not Satan have accused our Lord Jesus after He attained the age of knowing good and evil that He was responsible for the slaughter of those innocent male children in Bethlehem and its vicinity? Surely Satan would have brought grief to the heart of the Lord by citing this incident to Him. He would have constantly wounded the heart of our Lord that He was the cause of this horrible incident. That is why our Lord shows immeasurable love toward children. In Matthew 19:14 (NKJV), we read Jesus saying, "Let the little children come to Me and do not forbid them."

Beloved children of God, Satan should have thought our Lord Jesus would run away from the race which was ordained for Him when the wounds inflicted on Him by the piercing words of His enemies kept on pounding Him and the attack of Satan kept strangling His bleeding heart. But our Lord endured all these sufferings and trials for our sake and bore all our grief on the cross and finished His work of our salvation (John 19:28, 30).

Satan and his associates thought that they paid God back by wounding Jesus with their sneering, mockery, dishonor, and ridicule. But our Lord Jesus endured all the pain in His heart in order to save us also from the verbal attack of our enemies. "He was wounded for our transgressions, He was bruised for our iniquities; the chastisement for our peace was upon Him, and by His stripes we are healed" (Isa. 53:5, NKJV).

When our daughter went to be with the Lord, there were many who tried to destroy me and my ministry by their tongue-lashing. But our Lord placed some wonderful and notable friends in our lives at that point of time, who took all the verbal accusations on themselves and stood as a buffer between our enemies and us. There is one particular friend of mine who would not allow me to go to any place alone. He always stayed with me and took care of me. On the one side, he protected me from my enemies' attacks and on the other he comforted me and made me carry on our Lord's work. When a friend could do so much for me, my family, and ministry, how much more can our Lord Jesus who had Himself gone through all the pain on behalf of us, do for us in our lives?

Yes, when we are wounded and crushed by our enemies with despicable words, the Lord upholds us and rescues us. His Word says, "I will carry you; I will sustain you and I will rescue you" (Isa. 46:4, NIV). "He heals the brokenhearted and binds up their wounds" (Ps. 147:3, NIV).

It is the words of the enemies of Jesus that hurt our Lord's heart besides His physical sufferings. That is why our Lord sends His words to heal us. "He sent His word and healed them, and delivered them from their destructions" (Ps. 107:20, NKJV). It is the wounds of Jesus alone that can heal our broken hearts. "By His wounds you have been healed" (1 Pet. 2:24, NIV).

Chapter 12
WOUNDS ON HIS HANDS

For dogs have surrounded Me; the congregation of the wicked
has enclosed Me. They pierced My hands and My feet.
—PSALM 22:16, NKJV

The other disciples therefore said to him, "We have seen the
Lord." So he said to them, "Unless I see in His hands the
print of the nails, and put my finger into the print of the
nails, and put my hand into His side, I will not believe."
—JOHN 20:25, NKJV

SOME PEOPLE ALWAYS fail no matter what they attempt to do. So it is not surprising when others say to such a person, "You are not a lucky person!" "Nothing you touch ever seems to prosper!" "Please shy away from this endeavor!"

Recently I heard the testimony of a man who claimed that he was cursed. Everything he attempted to do ended in failure. He described how he became a partner in a business with another man. Within one week his business partner died. Another time he simply touched someone's brand new computer and the computer crashed beyond repair. The list of failures was nearly endless. Then one day someone told him about Jesus and he gave his life to the Lord. Eventually he entered full-time ministry and today everything he does is blessed.

Everyday we see the various ways that people make use of their hands. Some people use their hands to make a living such as breaking stones. There are others who use their hands to entertain us by performing various kinds of magical feats. Yet there are others who use their hands to harm society and those around them.

The same hands that are given to us by God can be used for good or evil. They can be a source of blessing or the cause of trouble depending on how they are used.

But consider the hands of our Lord Jesus. In every circumstance, the hands of Jesus proved a blessing to others. They gave healing, brought deliverance, and in every way, they were a source of blessing.

THE HAND OF JESUS
BRINGS HEALING

Beloved, while Jesus sojourned on this earth, lepers were treated as untouchables and kept isolated from the general population. In fact, they were not even allowed to enter into their own city, town, or village.

If by chance someone approached them, the lepers were to shout, "Unclean! Unclean!" in order to avoid contact with a healthy person. If they did not, they were stoned. One day, under these circumstances, a leper came running to Jesus. He said, "Lord Jesus, if you were willing, you can make me clean." Moved with compassion, Jesus put out His hand and touched Him saying, "I am willing; be cleansed." And immediately his leprosy was healed. As soon as the loving hand of Jesus touched the leper, whom society despised and whose flesh was decaying, he was immediately healed (Luke 5:12–13).

One day, Jesus went to the house of Simon Peter whose mother-in-law was lying sick with a fever. He took her by the hand and lifted her up, and immediately the fever left her and she served them (Mark 1: 30–31).

We see from this incident that the hand of Jesus not only brought healing to Peter's mother-in-law but also gave her strength, enabling her to get up from her sick bed and serve them. In the hand of Jesus, there is power to heal and renew.

THE HAND OF JESUS
BRINGS PROVISION

Once a great multitude followed Jesus into the wilderness. When he saw the people He was moved with compassion. Jesus took the five loaves of bread and two small fish given to Him in His hands.

He blessed the food and gave it to His disciples to distribute to the multitude. The Bible says on that day about five thousand men, besides women and children, ate and were filled (Matt. 14:15–21). In another instance, Jesus blessed seven loaves and a few little fish and fed four thousand men, and even more women and children (Matt. 15:32–34). Psalm 104:25–28 reveals that the hand of the Lord provides food to the innumerable creeping things, creatures both small and great in the sea. In the same way He provides the food to all animals (Ps. 104:14). The Bible also describes that the hand of the Lord created everything (Ps. 8:3; Gen. 2:7). His hand meets the needs of all created beings.

THE HAND OF JESUS
BRINGS BLESSING

While He sojourned on this earth, Jesus was very busy traveling from village to village preaching the good news of the kingdom of God. As He went about "doing good," multitudes followed Him.

One day, in the midst of His busy schedule, some women brought their children to be blessed by Jesus. When Jesus saw His disciples rebuking the mothers, He was greatly displeased and said to them, "Let the little children come to Me, and do not forbid them; for of such is the kingdom of God" (Mark 10: 14, NKJV).

Even His busy schedule could not prevent Jesus from blessing those little ones. He took them up in His arms, placed His hands on them, and blessed them (Mark 10:16).

The Bible says that after creating humans in His image and likeness, God blessed them saying, "Be fruitful and multiply; fill the earth and subdue it and have dominion over everything" (Gen. 1:27–28).

It is the nature of our God to bless His children. Our Lord Jesus Christ also demonstrated this same character of God while He was on this earth. He was always seen blessing people with His hands.

THE HANDS OF JESUS BRING HELP
IN TIMES OF TROUBLE

It was the fourth watch of the night, and Jesus' disciples were in a boat in the middle of the sea being tossed about by the waves. They were troubled when they saw Jesus walking on the water towards them. But Jesus spoke to them saying, "Be of good cheer, it is I, be not afraid."

Peter answered Him saying, "Lord, if it is you, command me to come to you on the water." Jesus said, "Come." And when Peter stepped out of the boat, he walked on the water to go to Jesus.

But while he was supernaturally walking on the water the boisterous wind distracted him, causing Peter to focus on his circumstances rather than on Jesus.

As he began to sink, Peter cried out, "Lord, save me!" Immediately Jesus stretched out His hand, caught him, and helped him to get back on the boat (Matt. 14:22–33).

My dearly beloved, the hand of Jesus is there to lift us up whenever we sink under the weight of the problems of this world. The hand of Jesus is the one that heals, creates, meets our needs, lifts us up, and blesses us.

REASON WHY HIS HANDS WERE PIERCED

Jeremiah 16:21 says, "Therefore, behold, I will this once cause them to know, I will cause them to know mine hand and my might; and they shall know that my name is The LORD." From this we can see that the hand of the Lord signifies the might and power of God.

The devil also knew that the might and power of God was released through the hands of Jesus. Working through the Roman soldiers, Satan attempted to stop the flow of God's power by binding the hands of Jesus to the cross with cruel nails.

But when the hands that had showered many blessings in the natural realm were nailed to the cross, there arose a significant flow of blessings in the spiritual realm. These spiritual blessings meet the essential needs of the people through the wounds in His hands.

Before I elaborate on how the wounds in Jesus' hands bring about blessings, let me show you certain things which are written against us and prove a hindrance to us in receiving God's blessings.

In Jeremiah 17:1, we see that the sin of Judah is written with a pen of iron and with the point of a diamond. These sins are deeply engraved upon the tablets of their hearts, and upon the horns of the altars. It is written in the most legible and indelible characters, never to be forgotten. This clearly shows our sins are not just embedded in our conscience but they are also written down in Satan's kingdom.

I believe that when we sin against God with our thoughts, words, and actions, we deserve punishment as they are contrary to the law of God. Besides this, Satan too has chalked out an evil plan to destroy us in his dispensation through means such as sorcery, witchcraft, palmistry, tarot cards, and the like.

Praise be to God as Colossians 2:14–15 (NKJV) says:

> Having wiped out the handwriting of requirements that was against us, which was contrary to us. And He has taken it out of the way, having nailed it to the cross. Having disarmed principalities and powers, He made a public spectacle of them, triumphing over them in it.

Jesus has totally disarmed principalities and powers.

Thus, the blood of Jesus shed from the wounds on His hands has wiped out our sins and has also canceled Satan's schemes and accusations, having nailed them all on the cross. Jesus has taken on the punishment that you and I rightly deserve.

Generally speaking, to revoke an existing law on record, a

higher authority needs to sign an order revoking the previous order issued by the lower authority.

So, to destroy and cancel what the devil, the "prince of this world" has written, Jesus who has all power in heaven and on earth, shed His blood as the ink, so to speak, for the signature that cancels all that has been written against us.

Therefore, we need not worry about the things that were written against us in the spiritual realm. The blood that flowed from the wounds on Jesus' hands blotted out all the written things and has given victory over the powers of darkness.

Before I came into the saving grace of Christ Jesus, I had once gone to see a palmist. Palm readers are people who claim to have special powers to foresee the future. At that time I didn't know that this was a form of witchcraft that the Bible forbids (Deut. 18:10).

The palm reader predicted that something terrible would happen to me, perhaps even death, around the age of twenty. It was when I was twenty years old that I wanted to commit suicide because of certain failures in my life. But my uncle told me about Jesus and how the wounds He suffered were for my salvation.

My uncle asked me to read Isaiah 53:5, which says, "But He was wounded for our transgressions, He was bruised for our iniquities; The chastisement for our peace was upon Him, And by His stripes we are healed" (NKJV). These powerful verses touched me profoundly, and I gave my life to the Lord.

I believe that the devil was trying to destroy me through the words of the palm reader. But the blood of Jesus blotted out the devil's plan and gave me a new life.

With the same nail-pierced hands, the risen Savior fed

His disciples who struggled all night without catching a single fish. With the same nail-pierced hands, the risen Lord blessed His disciples as He ascended into heaven, thereby proving that His nail-pierced hands bring provision and help to His children in times of trouble. Today He uses us as His healing hands.

The hands of our Lord bled when nailed to the cross, but they were never rendered powerless. They are the same powerful hands forever, blessing His children all the time.

Isaiah 49:16 (NKJV) says:

> See, I have inscribed you on the palms of my hands.

Since you are engraved on the nail-pierced hands of Jesus with the blood He shed for you, your future is *not* with the devil, but safe in the *hands* of the Lord, who created the heavens and the earth and the entire universe. Hallelujah!

Chapter 13
WOUNDS ON HIS FEET

And when they were come to the place, which is called
Calvary, there they crucified him, and the malefac-
tors, one on the right hand, and the other on the left.

—LUKE 23:33

For dogs have compassed me: the assembly of the wicked
have enclosed me: they pierced my hands and my feet.

—PSALM 22:16

THE ROMAN SOLDIERS took Jesus to a place called
Golgotha, which means "skull," and crucified Him
by nailing His hands and feet to the cross. If a few
nails are all that will have to hold up a person on the cross
you can imagine how tough and sharp they would have been.
This will give us an idea of the excruciating pain and deep
wounds the nails must have caused Jesus our Lord when they
were driven into His hands and legs. Dear ones, why did this
happen to Jesus? Why were His feet wounded and pierced
with nails?

TO SANCTIFY OR BEAUTIFY OUR FEET

We know from the Bible that "Jesus went about all the cities and villages, teaching in their synagogues, and preaching the gospel of the kingdom, and healing every sickness and every disease among the people. But when he saw the multitudes, he was moved with compassion for them, because they fainted, and were scattered abroad, as sheep having no shepherd" (Matt. 9:35–36).

Acts 10:38 reminds us, "How God anointed Jesus of Nazareth with the Holy Ghost and with power: who went about doing good, and healing all that were oppressed of the devil; for God was with him."

Dear readers, wherever He went while He sojourned on this earth, Jesus went about doing good. Here are just a few examples from the Bible.

> And he arose out of the synagogue, and entered into Simon's house. And Simon's wife's mother was taken with a great fever; and they besought him for her. And he stood over her, and rebuked the fever; and it left her: and immediately she arose and ministered unto them.
> —LUKE 4:38–39

> And when Jesus came to the place, He looked up and saw him, and said to him, "Zacchaeus, make haste and come down, for today I must stay at your house." So he made haste and came down, and received Him joyfully …And Jesus said to him, "Today salvation has come to this house, because he also is a son of Abraham."
> —LUKE 19:5–6, 9, NKJV

> Then when Jesus came, he found that he had lain in the grave four days already. And when he thus had

spoken, he cried with a loud voice, Lazarus, come forth. And he that was dead came forth, bound hand and foot with graveclothes: and his face was bound about with a napkin. Jesus saith unto them, Loose him, and let him go.

—JOHN 11:17, 43–44

And it came to pass, that, as the people pressed upon him to hear the word of God, he stood by the lake of Gennesaret, And saw two ships standing by the lake: but the fishermen were gone out of them, and were washing their nets. And he entered into one of the ships, which was Simon's, and prayed him that he would thrust out a little from the land. And he sat down, and taught the people out of the ship. Now when he had left speaking, he said unto Simon, Launch out into the deep, and let down your nets for a draught. And Simon answering said unto him, Master, we have toiled all the night, and have taken nothing: nevertheless at thy word I will let down the net. And when they had this done, they inclosed a great multitude of fishes: and their net brake. And they beckoned unto their partners, which were in the other ship, that they should come and help them. And they came, and filled both the ships, so that they began to sink.

—LUKE 5:1–7

And there are also many other things which Jesus did, the which, if they should be written every one, I suppose that even the world itself could not contain the books that should be written. Amen.

—JOHN 21:25

Therefore we can say that joy, peace, health, and blessings followed Jesus wherever He went. Psalm 23:6 says, "Surely goodness and mercy shall follow me all the days of my life; and I will dwell in the house of the LORD forever." In short, the people received and enjoyed His goodness.

On the other hand, confusion, strife, failure, disease, poverty, and all such unhappy things prevail wherever the devil abides. Since he is the prince of darkness, the places where he dwells are also full of darkness. But the places where Jesus and His Word abide will be bright with salvation and deliverance.

That is why the woman named Mary anointed the feet of Jesus with the costly ointment of spikenard. The following verses make this clear:

> Then took Mary a pound of ointment of spikenard, very costly, and anointed the feet of Jesus, and wiped his feet with her hair: and the house was filled with the odour of the ointment. Then saith one of his disciples, Judas Iscariot, Simon's son, which should betray him, Why was not this ointment sold for three hundred pence, and given to the poor?....Then said Jesus, Let her alone: against the day of my burying hath she kept this.
>
> —JOHN 12:3–5, 7

> She hath done what she could: she is come aforehand to anoint my body to the burying. Verily I say unto you, Wheresoever this gospel shall be preached throughout the whole world, this also that she hath done shall be spoken of for a memorial of her.
>
> —MARK 14:8–9

The word "gospel" means "good news." In Luke 4:18–19 Jesus says, "The Spirit of the Lord is upon me, because he hath anointed me to preach the gospel to the poor; he hath sent me to heal the brokenhearted, to preach deliverance to the captives, and recovering of sight to the blind, to set at liberty them that are bruised, To preach the acceptable year of the Lord."

This is indeed good news as God is ready to give His blessings to all that come to Him.

- To release people from the grip of poverty
- To give them prosperity
- To heal the broken-hearted
- To set the captives free
- To give sight to the blind

Our Lord and Savior Jesus Christ can do these things because He came to set people free. This is the good news of the gospel. To put it in a nutshell, there is a God who can deliver people from the clutches of the devil who wants to rule over them and hold them in captivity.

Preaching the gospel is nothing more than taking this good news of divine deliverance to people everywhere. We should declare that this is possible because our God is an Almighty (all-powerful) God who has complete authority over everything.

By anointing the feet of Jesus with the costly perfume, Mary revealed the honor, power, and authority that are due to Him. Whoever proclaims the authority of Jesus brings to remembrance this woman and the honor she gave to the Lord.

In Isaiah 66:1, the Lord declares, "Heaven is my throne

and the earth is my footstool" (NIV). This verse reveals the authority of God over all the earth that is symbolized by His feet.

In India, people bow and touch the feet of elders and dignitaries as a sign of respect and honor. In the same way people fell at the feet of Jesus in order to show their respect and honor for Him. Our God is indeed worthy of honor.

By nailing His feet to the cross, the devil believed that he could bring disgrace and dishonor to Jesus. But the blood that was shed from the wounds on His feet has made the feet of those who bring the gospel pure and beautiful.

Recorded in the thirteenth chapter of the book of John is the interesting account of Jesus washing the feet of His disciples. Washing the feet of a person prior to entering a house is a custom practiced in many eastern countries. The purpose is to remove the dust and dirt that has accumulated on the feet while walking on the road. This ritual must be performed every time a person goes out and comes in so as to keep him and the house clean.

When it was Peter's turn to have his feet washed, he refused. Jesus responded by telling Peter in that case he could have no part with Him. Peter then told the Lord to wash his hands and head also. Jesus replied, "He who is bathed needs only to wash his feet, but is completely clean; and you are clean" (John 13:10, NKJV). It is quite likely that the disciples had already bathed and only their feet were soiled and required rewashing after coming in contact with the dust and dirt of the road.

Symbolically, in order to keep the preacher of the gospel clean and pure, his feet must be washed. His entire body may have already been cleansed, but to remain clean and pure

Chapter 14
THE WOUND ON HIS SIDE

But one of the soldiers with a spear pierced his side,
and forthwith came there out blood and water.
—JOHN 19:34

JESUS WAS CRUCIFIED along with two other thieves on the eve of the Sabbath. According to Jewish law, the bodies of criminals should not remain on the cross on Sabbath Day, which was now drawing near. So it was customary to hasten death by breaking the bones of the criminals so that their bodies could be taken down and buried before the Sabbath.

Therefore the legs of the thieves crucified on either side of Jesus were broken. But when they came to break the legs of Jesus they discovered that He was already dead. Without breaking any of His bones, one of the soldiers thrust his spear into the side of Jesus to ensure that He was dead, and immediately blood and water came out.

Now the soldier could have pierced His thigh, His leg, or some other part of His body. Why did he choose His side in particular to pierce? As we have already explained, the devil inflicted each wound on the body of Jesus for a specific purpose and fulfilled his evil plans through the Jews and the Roman soldiers. So let us meditate on the basis of Scripture as to why the Roman soldier pierced His side.

The Last Drop of Blood Has Become the Foundation of the Church

The first time the word *church* is mentioned in the Bible is in Matthew 16:18: "And I also say to you that you are Peter, and on this rock I will build My church, and the gates of Hades shall not prevail against it" (NKJV). The phrase "I will build" implies that there could be no church until it was purchased by Christ's blood.

The Greek word for *church* is *ekklesia*. This word is used 115 times in the New Testament, mostly in the book of Acts, the writings of the apostle Paul, and the general epistles. On at least 92 occasions this word refers to a local congregation. The other references are to the church in general or to all believers everywhere, of all times.

When the church in general is implied, the term *church* refers to all who follow Christ, irrespective of locality and time. In other words the term *church* refers to the universal church.

I would like to point out a very interesting incident in the life of Jacob that seems to be a shadow (Col. 2:17) of the 'church' which Jesus mentioned in Matthew 16:18. While Jacob was going to Haran from Beersheba, fearing that his brother Esau might kill him, he took one of the stones of that place and put it under his head, and he lay down in that place to sleep. Then Jacob had a dream.

> And behold, the Lord stood above it and said: "I am the Lord God of Abraham your father and the God of Isaac; the land on which you lie I will give to you and your descendants. Also your descendants shall be as the dust of the earth; you shall spread abroad to the west and the east, to the north and the south; and in

you and in your seed all the families of the earth shall
be blessed. Behold, I am with you and will keep you
wherever you go, and will bring you back to this land;
for I will not leave you until I have done what I have
spoken to you."

Then Jacob awoke from his sleep and said, "Surely
the Lord is in this place, and I did not know it." And he
was afraid and said, "How awesome is this place! This
is none other than the house of God, and this is the
gate of heaven!"

Then Jacob rose early in the morning, and took the
stone that he had put at his head, set it up as a pillar,
and poured oil on top of it. And he called the name of
that place Bethel; but the name of that city had been
Luz previously. Then Jacob made a vow, saying, "If
God will be with me, and keep me in this way that I
am going, and give me bread to eat and clothing to put
on, so that I come back to my father's house in peace,
then the Lord shall be my God. And this stone which I
have set as a pillar shall be God's house, and of all that
You give me I will surely give a tenth to You."

—GENESIS 28:13–22

Here the stone which Jacob kept under his head signifies
our Lord Jesus Christ (Matt. 21:42, 44; Mark 12:10; Luke
20:17–18). When Jacob came in contact with that stone, he
had a revelation about his ancestral God and the covenant of
God. After he got up from sleep, he said, "This is the house
of God." Then he took the stone and set it as a pillar and
poured oil on top of it. Here Jacob was doing something
prophetically. He was painting a picture of how our Lord
Jesus would be lifted on the cross. We know that anointing
and blood go together (Lev. 8:30). When the last drop of

blood was shed from Jesus' side, it became the foundation of the heavenly pillar on earth, that is, the church. By anointing the stone with oil, Jacob also symbolically made it clear that after Jesus' ascension and the descending of the Holy Spirit, the church would come into existence.

THE REASON WHY JESUS' SIDE WAS PIERCED

We know that God formed man from the dust of the ground and breathed the breath of life into his nostrils. Not only that, God placed him in the Garden of Eden, which He Himself had planted.

> And the Lord God said, "It is not good that the man should be alone; I will make him an help meet for him." And the Lord God caused a deep sleep to fall upon Adam, and he slept: and he took one of his ribs, and closed up the flesh instead thereof, and the rib, which the Lord God had taken from man, made he a woman, and brought her unto the man.
>
> —GENESIS 2:18, 21–22

God opened Adam's side and removed a rib in order to form a wife for him. In other words, Adam's bride came from his side.

In Ephesians 5:22–32, we can see that Paul compares the husband and wife relationship with our Lord Jesus and the church—the church considered as the bride of Jesus. From the above, we can infer that symbolically the church is in the side of our Lord's flesh just as Eve was made from one of Adam's ribs on his side.

I strongly feel that the devil feared the bride of Christ, the church, symbolically positioned on His side. Because of this fear, the devil prompted the Roman soldier to pierce the side of Jesus.

We read in the Bible that as soon as His side was pierced blood oozed out and then water, too, flowed out. The last drop of blood was the seed of a new beginning.

> Most assuredly, I say to you, unless a grain of wheat falls into the ground and dies, it remains alone; but if it dies, it produces much grain.
>
> —JOHN 12:24, NKJV

Several years ago I listened to a sermon by a very famous preacher that moved me. He told of a missionary couple who came to Northeast India to work among the tribal people who lived in that area. But the tribal chief and his people were engaged in witchcraft and were totally against this couple.

In fact, they were very hostile towards them and on numerous occasions threatened to kill them. But this couple did not bother about these threats and continued their ministry among the people they loved. One of their achievements was teaching the tribal people the song "I Have Decided to Follow Jesus" by S. Sundar Singh:

> I have decided to follow Jesus;
> No turning back, no turning back.
> The world behind me, the cross before me;
> No turning back, no turning back.

One day the tribal chief told the missionary that if he did not stop singing this song they would kill his children. When he refused to comply with his order they tied him up and burned his children alive. While this was going on, the man continued singing, "I have decided to follow Jesus."

Then they told him that if he did not stop singing this song they would kill his wife. When he refused to oblige they burned his wife also alive. Still he continued singing, "I have decided to follow Jesus." Finally, they told him that if he did not stop singing this song they would kill him, too. But he continued singing, "I have decided to follow Jesus" until his last breath.

Most of the people in the village, including the chief, witnessed these events. They could not understand why these people willingly gave up their lives. Then the chief concluded that the God they were serving must be the one true God and he and the rest of the villagers decided to follow Jesus. Their deaths brought a great revival in that place, and today most of the people in that area are Christians as a result of the martyrdom of this missionary and his family.

One day while I was ministering in Malaysia, a gentleman asked me why there were so many preachers in the city of Chennai, previously known as Madras, India. The first thought that came to my mind that day was about the Apostle Thomas who came to Chennai in the first century. He brought the gospel of Jesus Christ all the way to India and became a martyr. I believe his death in Chennai was like a seed sown in the soil, which is now producing a great harvest of preachers.

In Acts 20:28, it is written, "…the church of God, which he hath purchased with his own blood." Once the last drop of blood was shed from the wound on His side, the bride (the church) came forth. Praise the Lord!

THE DEVIL TRIES TO DESTROY FAMILIES, JESUS SHED HIS BLOOD TO BUILD FAMILIES

There was another blessing, which resulted from the wound in His side.

God also established family bonds by creating Eve as a suitable help for Adam. It is His desire that the husband, wife, and children should live together as a family. Since this plan was formed in the mind of the Lord, we know that He has great concern for family life.

Today, the devil tries to destroy families by creating strife between husbands and wives that often leads to separation or infidelity. Due to this, people are sometimes caught in sin such as adultery and addiction to alcohol or gambling.

The bonds between parents and children have also been broken. Some children seldom obey their parents. They loaf around irresponsibly, often resulting in addictions to drugs and other evil habits. Thus the devil has ruined many families, destroying family order.

Jesus said:

> The thief does not come except to steal, and to kill, and to destroy.
> —JOHN 10:10, NKJV

The devil is a thief who steals the joy of family life, destroying the relationship between husband, wife, and children.

The devil intended to destroy families by inflicting a wound in the side of the One who first created family life. That last drop of blood that flowed from the side of Jesus was meant to give life and salvation to all members of the family.

Several years ago I met a young couple in the city of Dubai, UAE. The man told me that he was a Hindu by birth and did not want to have anything to do with Christians. But because he had a very successful business, many Christian families came to him seeking a marriage alliance for their daughters. Since he hated Christians he refused all offers.

Finally, he got engaged to a good Hindu girl. But after the engagement ceremony his fiancée told him that while she was in medical school she had accepted Jesus Christ as her personal Savior. She told him that after their marriage she wanted to continue her Christian faith. The man grew angry and wanted to break the engagement.

But he was hesitant to take such a drastic action because he had spent lavishly on the engagement ceremony. All his family members and relatives along with many business partners, politicians, and VIPs had attended the betrothal ceremony. Finally, he decided to marry the girl, but did not allow her to read her Bible or go to church after the marriage.

As time went by, many failures plagued his life, including the collapse of his business. This made him shift to a job overseas. He had lost peace of mind, but he was still stubborn towards his wife though she continued to shower her love on him.

One year on her birthday, she told her husband, "Honey, I would like a special gift from you this year." Thinking that she desired costly gold jewelry or some other expensive gift he replied, "Today I will give you whatever you desire." Immediately she requested that he attend a special church service with her. Since he had already given his word, he reluctantly went with her to the church.

From the moment they sat down, the power of God began to touch him. The man wept continually. Finally, the pastor came to speak to him, and the man willingly gave his life to the Lord. Today he has a successful career, his entire family has come into the salvation experience, and he is now serving the Lord.

God's promise in Acts 16:31 is true. "Believe on the Lord Jesus Christ, and you will be saved, you and your household" (NKJV). The blood that Jesus shed from the wound in His side has the power to save you and your household.

The last drop of blood that oozed out from His side can bring love, joy, peace, and healthy relationships in our families. Jesus is the only One who can give us abundant life.

Yes! Beloved! The devil tried to destroy churches and families by inflicting wounds on His side. But the blood of Jesus that flowed out from His side is the foundation for His bride, the church, and has brought salvation, joy, and peace into families. Hallelujah!

Chapter 15
TEARING HIS HUMAN BODY

*Therefore, brethren, having boldness to enter the Holiest by
the blood of Jesus, by a new and living way which He conse-
crated for us, through the veil, that is, His flesh.*

—HEBREWS 10:19–20, NKJV

W HEN OUR LORD Jesus Christ gave up His spirit,
the veil of the temple was torn in two from top
to bottom (Matt. 27:50–51). This event of the
spirit of Lord Jesus Christ leaving His body is depicted in
Hebrews 10:19–20. His spirit departing from His body signifies His physical death.

In the Garden of Eden, God had commanded Adam and
Eve not to eat from the tree of the knowledge of good and
evil, for on the day they ate of that tree they would surely
die (Gen. 2:17). But they disobeyed His command and ate
the forbidden fruit. According to God's declaration, Adam
and Eve should have died on the day they ate the fruit, but
they lived on for many years in this world. Now the question
arises why Adam and Eve did not die immediately when they
disobeyed God's command.

Let us look into God's revelation concerning seemingly
contradictory things. Adam and Eve were living in God's
presence in the Garden of Eden. However, deceived by Satan,
they ate the fruit of the forbidden tree. Then they both heard

the sound of the Lord God as He was walking in the cool of the day. They feared to remain in His presence, so they hid themselves.

Since both Adam and Eve sinned, God drove them out of the Garden of Eden. Thus their communion with God was cut off. In other words, on the day they sinned by eating the fruit, they had a spiritual death. Later they experienced physical death. In brief, being cast out of God's presence is spiritual death, which God spoke of in Genesis 2:17; physical death takes place when a man's spirit leaves his body.

Bible scholars think that the description in Isaiah 14:12–14 and Ezekiel 28:12–17 portrays the sins of Lucifer and his downfall. A comparative study of the two passages shows the type of sins Lucifer might have committed.

Satan, who was created by God, was called the morning star and the son of dawn. He was appointed as the guardian cherub. Satan became proud on account of his beauty and his riches. His wisdom was corrupted because of his splendour. He said to himself as in Isaiah 14:13, "I will ascend to heaven, I will raise my throne above the stars of God" (NKJV). To this day, man has not been able to number the stars in the Milky Way galaxy. But Satan said that he would raise his throne high above all the creation of God. He aspired to reign over everything, leaving his God-given job and his responsibilities.

Furthermore, Satan said in his heart, "I will sit enthroned on the mount of assembly on the utmost heights of the saved mountain" (Isa. 14:13, NKJV). Only our God is worthy to be worshiped. Satan thought the created beings should leave the Creator God, and instead worship him, the created being. He also said in his heart, "I will ascend to heaven, and become equal with God."

When Satan wanted to become equal to the most high

God and had corrupted God's holy place, he was thrown down from the holy mountain, that is, from God's presence. This denotes his spiritual death.

Adam and Eve were sent out because they sinned. Likewise Lucifer was also driven out from God's presence. Spiritual death took place for Lucifer when he was pushed down from God's presence. That's why the devil is said to be the ruler of death (Heb. 2:14). When a person enters a totally uninhabited island he becomes virtually the monarch of all he surveys. Similarly when Satan entered the realm of death as the very first person to do so, it may be presumed that he appropriated this authority over death. The Scripture says, "For the wages of sin is death" (Rom. 6:23) because sin brought death to humanity.

When our Lord Jesus Christ came to this world, the devil tried all his means to kill Jesus, and the devil thought that by His death he could then become the lord over even Jesus Christ. That is why the devil tried to destroy Jesus from His very birth, and he devised many plans to kill Jesus by inducing men. But he could not do any harm to Jesus.

In the garden of Gethsemane, when Jesus gave Himself up to God's will, the devil tormented Jesus using the Roman soldiers, and Jesus underwent great physical torture. He was grievously wounded and left with the soldiers to be killed. The devil thought Jesus would die there because He was beaten, scourged, and struck so many times; He would have bled profusely and could have died.

We read very often in the newspaper about deaths caused by accidents. For example, a man stumbled on a stone and died immediately because he fell down on the ground and suffered head injuries. I had a friend who was a pastor. One day when he was out riding on a motorbike, he smashed into a tractor and his legs were fractured. As he had lost a lot of blood from his body, he died while he was being taken to the hospital. When people die like this due to profuse bleeding and being hit on their bodies, why is it that our Lord did not die even after He was beaten, whipped, and His whole body was torn, resulting in profuse bleeding?

Now I share with you what the Spirit of God revealed to me when I was meditating upon our Lord's death. The Scripture says, "For the wages of sin is death" (Rom. 6:23). If a man does not commit sin, will he yet die? Today, some people say that our Lord led a secret sinful life. If our Lord had led a sinful life, I believe He would have died when the Roman soldiers whipped Him mercilessly. But "In Him is no sin" (1 John 3:5). "He committed no sin and no deceit was found in His mouth" (1 Pet. 2:22, NIV). Because He had no sin in Him, I believe, though He was beaten fiercely many times continually and every part of His body was tortured, He did not die then. But He experienced excruciating pain.

His torture is depicted in Psalm 22:14–16. "I am poured out like water, and all my bones are out of joint: my heart is like wax; it is melted in the midst of my bowels. My strength is dried up like a potsherd; and my tongue cleaveth to my jaws; and thou hast brought me into the dust of death. For dogs have compassed me: the assembly of the wicked have enclosed me: they pierced my hands and my feet."

We can find many verses similar to the following: "Because he himself suffered when he was tempted, he is able to help those who are being tempted" (Heb. 2:18, NIV). Though Jesus went through indescribable sufferings, He did not die. From this we can understand that our Lord was sinless. Satan, the prince of death, wanted to pluck the life from Jesus. But He could not take the life of Jesus because Jesus did not commit any sin. Even before Jesus went to the cross, and gave up His life there, He told His disciples, "Therefore doth my Father love me, because I lay down my life, that I might take it again. No man taketh it from me, but I lay it down of myself. I have power to lay it down, and I have power to take it again. This commandment have I received of my Father" (John 10:17–18). No one had the power to take life from Jesus. He was powerful enough to lay down His life and regain His life.

Satan devised many plans to smite Jesus through people and crucify Him in order to kill Him. But our Lord laid down His life on His own so that we could have victory over death, which was and is the result of our sin. Since Jesus had no sin in Him, death could not have any hold on Him. For the atonement of our sins, Jesus gave Himself up not only to be smitten, but He also offered His life on the cross.

Thus by allowing His body to be torn, Jesus opened up a way for humans, who were sent away from God's presence, to return to the holy place. The prince of death could not enslave Jesus since He did not have any sin.

God raised our Lord Jesus Christ from death on the third day by His Spirit, and thus Jesus Christ had victory over the last enemy that is death. "The last enemy to be destroyed is death" (1 Cor. 15:26, NIV). "Where, O death, is your victory? Where, O death, is your sting? The sting of death is sin and the power of sin is the law. But thanks be to God! He gives us the victory through our Lord Jesus Christ" (1 Cor. 15:55–57, NIV).

Beloved readers, our Lord Jesus has made a way for us to have eternal life, the privilege of going to heaven, and also we can enter into the holy of holies where God's dwelling place is. At the same time He can dwell in our hearts through His sufferings and His death. This is a great blessing for us.

When their end comes, some men lament, "Alas! I go leaving my riches!"; "I go leaving my loved ones!"; "I go leaving my authority!" Some people die crying, "Alas! It's very dark!"; "I am afraid of death!"

Proverbs 24:20 says, "For the evil man has no future hope" (NIV). But how will the end of a righteous man be? The mother of a friend of mine once fell sick and was admitted to a hospital. One day while she was in her sick bed, she called her husband and asked him to read Psalm 23. When her husband read the last verse, "Surely goodness and mercy shall follow me all the days of my life; And I will dwell in the house of the Lord forever," she repeated the same verse and closed her eyes and died peacefully. "Mark the perfect man, and behold the upright: for the end of that man is peace" (Ps. 37:37). The Scripture says, "We have now been justified by his blood" (Rom. 5:9, NIV).

According to Isaiah 64:6, man cannot stand righteous before the holy God. Physical death can take place in a man any time and in any way. But when a man accepts Lord Jesus as the Son of God and as his Lord and Savior and believes on Him, then his physical death becomes a door for him to enter into heaven and he will never die.

Jesus said, "I am the resurrection, and the life: he that believeth in Me, though he were dead, yet shall he live: And whosoever liveth and believeth in Me shall never die" (John 11:25–26). Satan thought that he could become the ruler of Jesus by killing Him. But the Lord Jesus *tasted* death for everyone so as to redeem us from death (Heb. 2:9). Through His death on the cross, the Lord Jesus Christ made known to us a way to enter into the holy place of God. Beloved readers, accept this way and become the privileged citizens of heaven. Hallelujah!

Chapter 16
AGONY IN THE GARDEN

*And being in an agony [of mind] He prayed [all the] more
earnestly and intently, and His sweat became like great
clots of blood dropping down upon the ground.*

—LUKE 22:44, AMP

RECENTLY ON MY television program that is broad-
cast across South Asia and the Middle East, I gave
a series of teachings about the wounds of Jesus.
Many people wrote to me saying how they were touched and
blessed by these teachings. One lady in particular mentioned
that she appreciated knowing these deep spiritual truths, and
then went on to ask me a question.

She wanted to know the reason why Jesus sweated great
drops of blood in the Garden of Gethsemane. I found this
question interesting since I did not address this subject at
all in any of the television programs. After reading her letter
I began to ponder and pray about it. In this chapter I will
share with you what the Lord revealed to me.

Some time back one of my father's old friends asked me,
"Are you the son of Mr. Ebenezer?" Surprised by the question I responded, "Yes!" and then I asked him, "How were
you able to recognize me?" He replied, "Your way of doing
things is just like your father's." He said, "When I look at you
I can see your father."

He was right. My characteristics and mannerisms are just like those of my father. My father has passed these traits and attributes down to me. In the same way, when I look at my son I can see myself. He has the same mannerisms and characteristics that I have. It is like this with every generation. My son is like me. I am like my father. My father is like my grandfather.

As I thought about this I realized that some of the traits and attributes that we have could be traced back through the generations, all the way back to our common ancestors Adam and Eve. That means all of us possess some common characteristics.

But what do we all have in common? It was then that the Holy Spirit impressed upon my heart that the common trait we all have is disobedience. We have inherited our rebellious nature from Adam and Eve.

When He walked this earth, Jesus was 100 percent God and 100 percent man. Hebrews 2:17 (NKJV) says:

> Therefore, in all things He had to be made like His brethren, that He might be a merciful and faithful High Priest in things pertaining to God, to make propitiation for the sins of the people.

And the genealogy of Jesus, which is recorded in Luke 3:23–38, can be traced all the way back to Adam. Could it be that "disobedience," the common trait that all of us have inherited from Adam, was trying to overcome Jesus in the Garden of Gethsemane?

The word *Gethsemane* means "an oil press." I visited the Garden of Gethsemane several years ago during my tour of the Holy Land. While I was there I saw olive trees that must have been descendants from the ancient grove. At one time, as the name suggests, there must have been an oil press there to squeeze oil from the olives. Even though the press is long gone, the name remains the same.

I believe that it was here at Gethsemane that the ruler of this world pressed Jesus to disobey God, like he tempted Jesus in the wilderness. Jesus knew that He came into this world destined for the cross, to make propitiation for the sins of humankind. The One who has no beginning and no end had to die.

In the Amplified Bible Mark 14:33 says:

> And He took with Him Peter and James and John, and began to be struck with terror and amazement and deeply troubled and depressed.

In the garden, Jesus was struck with terror and amazement; He was deeply troubled and depressed. The word *terror* means "intense fear." Jesus, who had not yet faced suffering and death, was now confronted with the reality of what was about to happen to Him. His state of mind was that of terror in the initial moments leading up to the start of the actual events.

Imagine the doctor informs you about the details of your medical condition before it actually manifests in your body. For example, the lesion on your arm turns out to be skin cancer. Your initial reaction may be that of fear until you remember that Jesus has already paid the price for your healing. Are you going through the valley of fear today?

Remember Jesus was also struck with the terror and knows what you are going through. Hebrews 4:15 (NKJV) reminds us:

For we do not have a High Priest who cannot sympathize with our weaknesses, but was in all points tempted as we are, yet without sin.

The previous verse says that Jesus was struck with amazement. *Amazement* is the condition of being filled with great surprise. Although Jesus already knew that He would have to suffer and die on the cross, the actual events were now suddenly upon Him.

Consider visiting your loved ones during the holidays and all of a sudden you realize that tomorrow is the last day of your visit. Even though you knew it was coming, the day of your departure came very quickly. In life you may be faced with sudden occurrences that shock and amaze you. Remember that Jesus knows exactly what you are facing.

The verse says that Jesus was deeply troubled. *Deeply troubled* also means "greatly disturbed." Jesus was greatly disturbed in the moments prior to His suffering and death. He endured the agony of this state of mind. When someone disturbs your life, your work, or your routine, you may become annoyed or irritated. Jesus knows the suffering that you are going through and will help you.

Hebrews 2:18 (NKJV) says:

For in that He Himself has suffered, being tempted, He is able to aid those who are tempted.

Finally, this scripture reveals that Jesus was depressed. *Depressed* means "gloomy, dejected, or causing sadness."

Jesus was probably sad that He would soon have to leave His beloved disciples and that Judas was about to betray Him.

Because of all these things, terror, amazement, troubled state, and depression, His agony and emotional stress became so great that blood came forth from His skin. Surprisingly, this is a documented medical condition. As Dr. C. Truman Davis explains:

> The physical passion of Christ began in Gethsemane. Of the many aspects of this initial suffering the one, which is of particular physiological interest, is the bloody sweat.
>
> Interestingly enough, the physician Luke is the only evangelist to mention this occurrence. He says, "And being in an agony, and his blood, tricking down upon the ground." (Luke 22:44)
>
> Every attempt imaginable has been used by modern scholars to explain away the phenomenon of bloody sweat, apparently under the mistaken impression that it simply does not occur. A great deal of effort could be saved by consulting the medical literature.
>
> Though very rare, the phenomenon of hematidrosis, or bloody sweat, is well documented. Under great emotional stress, tiny capillaries in the sweat glands can break, thus mixing blood with sweat. This process alone could have produced marked weakness and possible shock.[1]

While Satan was tempting Him in the Garden of Gethsemane to disobey God, Jesus prayed, "Father, if it is Your will,

---

1 Dr. C. Truman Davis, "The Crucifixion of Jesus Christ: A Medical Explanation of What Jesus Endured on the Day He Died," *Arizona Medicine*, March 1965.

take this cup away from Me; nevertheless not My will, but Yours, be done" (Luke 22:42, NKJV).

He did not disobey God, and because of the great agony and emotional stress Jesus was going through, He sweated great drops of blood. He shed His blood in order to save us from terror, amazement, troubled states, depression, and emotional stress. Are you struck with any or all these things? The blood of Jesus that was shed in the garden of Gethsemane has the power to bring you peace and rest. He who has Himself endured the agony will help you. Jesus said, "Come to Me, all you who labour and are heavy laden, and I will give you rest" (Matt. 11:28). At the same time, the blood of Jesus which was shed in the garden of Gethsemane will also impart the obedience of Jesus in you, so that you can obey God and His commandments.

Conclusion

For the preaching of the cross is to them that perish foolish-
ness; but unto us who are saved it is the power of God.
—1 Corinthians 1:18

ATAN MUST HAVE rejoiced as he watched Jesus Christ, the Son of God, being crucified on the cross. He was probably thinking that every plan of God had finally been thwarted. He must have been thinking there was no way that Jesus would ever return from the cross to bless, deliver, and comfort His people.

Satan and his accomplices had knowledge, but they lacked wisdom. For had they known what God knew, they would have never crucified Him.

First Corinthians 2:7–8 (NKJV) says:

> But we speak the wisdom of God in a mystery, even the hidden wisdom, which God ordained before the world unto our glory: Which none of the princes of this world knew: for had they known it, they would not have crucified the Lord of glory.

Jesus defeated all the plans of the devil on the cross. All of the sufferings, all of the wounds, and all of the pain that Jesus experienced on the cross have become the power of God to us. We are now able to overcome any hurdle and prevail over everything because of this divine power that is within us.

After His resurrection, Jesus told the disciple Thomas to put his fingers in His wounds. They were healed, yet they were still there and could be seen, touched, and felt. Perhaps the wounds of Jesus are still visible on His body today. The scars on Jesus' body are the only manmade things in heaven.

In the 1980s I played competitive field hockey at the national level. Every game was an intense physical battle, especially among rival colleges and universities. It was not uncommon for players to receive several bruises and cuts requiring sutures in every match. In spite of these injuries, we played on and battled to win some of these matches.

Today I have many scars on my body. I call still look at them and tell you where and when I received each scar and whether or not we won the match. Now if every scar on my body can speak like that, then think about the scars on the body of our Lord Jesus Christ.

Once upon a time there was a couple vacationing on a cruise ship. The woman was very beautiful, but the man she was married to had terrible scars all over his face. Everyone on the ship was looking at them and wondering why they were together. Finally, one old man approached the beautiful woman and asked her about the man with the scarred face. She explained that the man was her husband. The old man then asked why she had married such an ugly man.

The woman immediately began to cry and told him that when she was a little girl there was a fire in her house. In the midst of the flames she cried out for help, but no one would come to her rescue. Finally, one young man heard her cries for help and went in to save her. He was the only one willing to come to her aid.

But while he was carrying the little girl out of the burning house, there was an explosion which burned his face beyond recognition. Now the little girl's father was a rich man and paid all of the young man's hospital bills. When he was well enough to leave the hospital, he sent him some money.

Years passed and it was time for the girl to get married. She told her father that her desire was to marry the man who saved her life. The father responded by telling her that the man had probably forgotten all about her. She told her father that the man could never forget her because every time he looked into a mirror he would think of her. The father finally agreed and began searching for the man. They eventually got married and lived happily ever after.

Similarly, when Jesus sees the scars on His body, they remind Him of us and how they are the cause of bringing salvation, freedom, peace, healing, and joy in our lives.

Jesus took upon Himself the entire punishment for all of the sins that we commit—in our mind, by our eyes, ears, mouth, hands, legs, and body—against Him and every part of His body.

Also, when the devil comes to accuse us, Jesus can show the wounds on His body as proof and remind him that He had paid the full price for our forgiveness and blessing.

By receiving the wounds from the crown of His head to the soles of His feet, Jesus in fact "took up our infirmities and carried our diseases" as is said in Matthew 8:17 (NIV). The stripes (scars) on the body of the resurrected Christ (that bring about healing for us) stand proof of the fact that He carried our diseases on His body.

As I mentioned earlier, when my father met with a terrible accident, the words in the title of this book began speaking to me and rekindling my faith. I believe with all my heart that Jesus paid the price for our peace, health, and blessing through His sufferings.

Every day while my father was in the hospital, I sat at his bedside going over the first draft of this book over and over again. Occasionally my father would wail and cry out in pain. The doctor told us that a CT scan must be performed because of the injury on his head. While I consented to this, I continued to believe in my heart that by the stripes of Jesus my father was healed.

Because of my father's memory loss, the doctors were afraid that there might be a skull fracture and that blood and fluid might have entered the brain. They wanted to get a second opinion from a neurosurgeon, to which I agreed. But I continued believing in my heart that my father was healed by the stripes of Jesus.

The specialist came and examined my father thoroughly. He came to the conclusion that even though my father was seventy-five years old and had fallen down eighteen steps, there was no injury to his brain. Other than the bumps and bruises and the weakness in his body from significant blood loss there were no permanent injuries.

During my father's recovery I sat at his bedside pondering over this book and continually confessing that my father was healed by the stripes of Jesus. Due to the prayers of many and our faith, my father was completely healed. He could sit and walk properly. He was able to recognize his children and our mother. He could carry on an intelligent conversation. Years later he died due to natural causes.

And we continue to confess that he was healed by the stripes of Jesus. After all, only the wounds of Jesus can bring true happiness, peace, health, and blessing. My dear reader, I believe that you, too, can receive these blessings in your life as I have received in mine. For we surely know that the devil has been defeated. Not only that, when we understand the spiritual message revealed by the wounds of Jesus we will be thankful to Him throughout our lives in addition to enjoying the blessings He earned for us on the cross.

I pray that God will give us His grace to enjoy the blessings earned by Jesus on the cross, so that we lead a victorious Christian life, offering praises and thanksgiving to Him all the days of our lives.

A Prayer for You

Dear gracious and loving heavenly Father,

I thank You for sending Your only begotton Son as a propitiation for all my sins. I fully understand the extent of humiliation Your Son had to undergo on my behalf. I also realize how much excruciating pain He would have endured on the cross as the price for my redemption from sin leading to eternal condemnation and thus to give me life and blessings—both material and spiritual. Having understood these facts, I totally surrender my life to You. Forgive all my sins and cleanse me by the blood of Jesus Christ. Come into my heart and abide in me. Please write my name in the Book of Life.

Lord, I understand that You also came into this world to destroy the works of the devil. Deliver me from oppression and depression. Set me free from all bondages of Satan. By Your mercy, give me the strength to walk in victory.

I thank You, Lord, for carrying all my weaknesses and sickness in Your body. Your stripes stand as a proof that You have suffered in order to heal me. Heal all my sicknesses. Give me perfect health, both physical and mental.

Remember the wounds on the side of Jesus Christ and save all my family members. Help me to serve You as a family. May Your peace rest in my heart, in my family, and in my works. Grant me the grace to always glorify Your name.

Bless me so that I will be a blessing to others. Give me the assurance of eternal life and its fullness. All praise, glory, and honor to You alone. In Jesus' matchless name I pray, Amen.

> If you have been blessed by this book, introduce
> this book to others, and be a blessing.

To Contact the Author

Showers of Blessing
Post Bag No. 5103
Chennai – 600 094 India
Prayer line: 91-44-65853066
Tel / Fax: 91-44-28487745
E-mail: samuelmohanraj@gmail.com
Website: www.sobm.com

Contact Address in America
211 Bay Shore Rd.
Bay Shore, NY 11706
631-665-5241 (Rev. John D. Johnson)